I Never Said Goodbye

A Mother's Memoir of Love and Brutal Loss Inside Saddam's Regime

Pauline Knowles-Samarraie

with Karen O'Brien

André Deutsch

First published in Great Britain in 2007 by

André Deutsch
an imprint of the
Carlton Publishing Group
20 Mortimer Street
London W1T 3JW

A catalogue record for this book is available from the British Library.

ISBN: 978-0-233-00211-8

Typeset by E-Type, Liverpool
Printed and bound in Great Britain by Mackays

Contents

1. Baghdad Bound

We watched in disbelief as the black-and-white television images told the bloody story of a military coup in my future husband's homeland, Iraq. Early on July 14, 1958, troops led by a group within the military calling itself the Free Officers poured into the capital, Baghdad, where they occupied strategic buildings including the radio station. There, one of the coup leaders, Abdul Salem Aref, broadcast to the Iraqi masses that the military was now in control, the monarchy had fallen and Iraq had become a republic. He declared that the army had 'liberated the beloved homeland from the corrupt crew that imperialism had installed' – a reference to the Hashemite monarchy and to Britain, the former colonial power, which had enthroned Iraq's first king, Faisal, in 1921.

I turned from the television screen to my fiancé, Munem. His face was ashen as he looked helplessly at what was happening in his birthplace, thousands of miles away from my small living room in Birmingham, in the English Midlands.

The royal palace in Baghdad had come under heavy bombardment. The young king, Faisal II, and other members of the royal family, women and children among them, had emerged to certain death. Moments after fleeing the buildings, and seemingly abandoned to their fate, they lay dead, shot repeatedly by the troops waiting outside. The King was just 23. He had succeeded to the throne in 1939 as a very young child, after his father, King Ghazi, was killed in a car crash, and now barely into his twenties, he too was dead. King Faisal's body was later taken away for a decent burial at a location that was kept secret to prevent it becoming a place of pilgrimage for monarchists who might try to challenge the new leadership. The monarchy had become deeply unpopular with its people and now the old order had been destroyed in a hail of gunfire and in the bloody aftermath of the coup many hundreds of Iraqis were being killed.

The body of the King's uncle, Abdul Ilah, who had been Regent until Faisal was old enough to rule, was taken from the palace grounds and tied to the back of a car. From there, it was dragged through the streets to the delight of the bloodthirsty mob. His remains were eventually taken for all to see, to the Ministry of Defence – a powerful symbolic gesture because this was where the bodies of four colonels hanged for taking part in a revolt in 1941 had been displayed as a deterrent to others. It was later announced that the Prime Minister, Nuri Said, had been captured and shot dead. It was said that his killers reversed their vehicle over his body several times. Later, after his burial, to heap further indignity upon his memory, his body was exhumed from the grave and mutilated.

'Munem!' I could barely form the words to describe such chaos and brutality, let alone comprehend what this bloody turn of events would mean for us and our future. We were to be married in a few months' time and would eventually be living in Iraq. I could see Munem was still digesting the news but I needed to know: 'Munem, how can we ever go to Iraq now?' The answer to that question came exactly four years later. I was on board an Iraqi Airways aircraft and sleeping beside me was our three-year-old son, Mazin. That midsummer day saw us heading for Baghdad at long last, almost a year after Munem had returned to Iraq. He'd completed his studies at Birmingham University, where he'd graduated with a Bachelor's degree in chemical engineering. Like many of the most promising young Iraqis of his generation, he'd had the benefit of a government-funded education abroad and now was expected to play a strong role in helping to build the new, modern Iraqi nation. He'd gone back to Iraq to complete his training as an officer in the army and to find a home for us in Baghdad. We were going to be reunited as a family.

My last two days in England had passed in a blur of frenetic activity and preparation. My mother and I had parted in tears when Mazin and I said goodbye to her. We'd been staying with her in Halifax, the West Yorkshire town in the north-west of England, where I'd grown up. When Munem went back to Iraq, Mazin and I had moved in with her and it had been so good to spend that time together. By the time I left England, Mum had been a widow for four years. She and my father had been inseparable from the day they were married and she still felt his loss very deeply. I felt guilty at leaving her, both of us trying to comfort ourselves and each other with the thought that my place was with my husband and that Mazin needed to be with his Daddy. Mum assured me that she would be kept busy back home and that I was not to worry about her. She was still working, which would be a good distraction from missing us too much, and she had the family – her two sisters and two brothers – who would keep an eye on her for me. When Munem and I had married four years earlier, it must have crossed my parents' minds that this day would come. I suppose they felt at the time that they would be facing it together. They were such private people that they kept their innermost fears and worries to themselves and, if they had concerns about me marrying a man from another culture and religion, they never expressed them.

I know they were sad when Munem and I moved to Birmingham but they'd never have tried to stop me going. Besides, they knew how strong-willed I was and that I'd have gone anyway if I'd already made up my mind to do it. As an only child, I was used to being my own person and making my own decisions. Like mothers the world over, one of Mum's stock phrases was 'You make your bed, you lie in it!' She'd always say that whatever you decide to do in your life, stick with it – make your decision, then follow it through to the end. As we hugged for one last time, I said through my tears, 'You will come to visit me from time to time. Mum, you *must* come to visit me!' The thought of having her with me in Iraq was a real comfort and made the goodbyes just a tiny bit easier.

Mazin and I boarded the train that took us south and, several hours later, we arrived at King's Cross station in London. From there, we got the Underground out to Heathrow airport on the western fringes of the city. I didn't quite know what to expect at the airport – I'd never even been to one before that day – but I didn't think the various check-in and customs procedures would be too much bother. My first-ever passport was safely tucked away in my handbag. I was going to be travelling by plane for the first time in my life. At Heathrow I was going to meet up with a friend, Barbara, who'd be my travelling companion on the flight to Baghdad. She too was joining her Iraqi husband. We'd been friends for four years in Birmingham, where our husbands had been students together on their chemical engineering course. The check-in procedures went smoothly and Mazin and I went through to the departure lounge. I looked around for Barbara but couldn't see her and her young daughter anywhere. But I did recognise one very familiar face – sitting at the bar was the comedian Tommy

Cooper, one of the best-known figures in British television light entertainment at the time. His quiet demeanour was so at odds with his gregarious stage persona. It seemed suddenly surreal to be seeing this larger-than-life character from the world of TV perched on a bar-stool only a few feet away from me. So this is what international travel was like!

At the bar, I ordered a Babycham and in my mind, raised a toast in farewell to my old life and in welcome anticipation of the one that was about to begin. I sipped it slowly, savouring the taste and the bubbles, and watching everything around me − all kinds of people crowded here together, some milling around, others strolling to fill in the time, some looked bored and others excited, so many of us just waiting, some perhaps at the edge of a brave new beginning like me, and others perhaps leaving behind a part of their lives, watching it draw to a close. Then I heard the boarding call for our flight come across the loud-speaker. I gathered up Mazin; he'd been such a good little boy, playing with his toy car on the carpet, and delighting in the discovery that he could make the automatic doors open and close simply by stepping this way or that in front of them. He was only three but he was so bright and quick to learn; his vocabulary was that of a five-year-old and I was surprised at times by how grown-up and self-assured he was. Mazin seemed to sense that this was a big adventure for him too but he wasn't in the least unsettled by all the activity. Now, it really was time to go.

Once we were inside the Iraqi Airways plane, I noticed that it was only half-full so there'd be plenty of room to stretch our legs and walk around later without disturbing people. We made our way to our seats, where Barbara and her daughter were already settled in. It was so lovely to see her again after a year, during which she'd stayed in Birmingham with her young daughter, and Mazin and I had gone up to Halifax to Mum. Barbara was only 21 but she seemed older, more mature in many ways because she was so calm. She had such a nice way about her that just being around her never failed to relax me, so she was the perfect companion for my first flight. While we had lots of catching up to do, we knew that could wait. We were so exhausted after the day's travelling that we simply settled the children and tried to relax ourselves. The flight attendant gave Mazin some crayons and a colouring book and, as he busied himself happily with those, I just gave in to the wave of tiredness that overcame me. The book I'd brought with me dropped open on my lap and I slipped into sleep, lulled by the hypnotic drone of the engines. When I awoke, I felt better – not totally refreshed but the nap had taken the edge off my exhaustion. Meals were served – a choice of chicken and rice or roast beef and potatoes. I opted for the latter, thinking that the traditional British fare would be a contrast to the kind of food I'd probably have to get used to in Iraq.

I looked out of the window at the endless sky around us and thought of the moment that had led me to this. I was

18, a student nurse at Halifax General Hospital. On a day off, my friend Hazel, who was also on the course, had come with me to a popular pub in town. Its name – The Old Cock – was, predictably, a source of many jokes but, the double entendres aside, it was a fun place and, on the few occasions when we could forget about our studies and our twelve-hour shifts, we'd meet friends there. The bar was nicely decorated with flock wallpaper and, best of all, mirrors everywhere so you could always have a quick check that your make-up was still looking good and, just as important, take a sneaky peek at who else might be in the bar. We arrived early this particular evening and ordered our favourite tipple, the fashionable drink that all the girls wanted to be seen sipping, Babychams. Lounge-bar music was playing, classics like Glenn Miller and 'Moonlight Serenade', but the bar was still almost empty so, with little else to distract us, it didn't take long to notice the two gorgeous young men seated at the other end of the room.

I looked at Hazel and she at me. We were clearly both thinking the same thing: 'They're a bit of all right, aren't they, Hazel?' She nodded and, trying to disguise the fairly obvious fact that we'd noticed them and were now discussing them, she said, 'But which one do you like?' I didn't even hesitate. 'I like the one with the black trousers and black-and-white sports jacket; the one with the very thick black hair. That one, tall with the big brown sexy eyes!' Appropriately enough, the song playing at that moment was

Frank Sinatra singing the Cole Porter classic, 'I've Got You Under My Skin'. So for the next hour or so, the two young men watched us watching them watching us. But that was as far as it went and, eventually, Hazel and I had to be getting home. As we reluctantly walked away up the street to catch the bus, I felt a tap on my shoulder. I spun around and my heart started pounding – it's such a cliché but it really was that surge of excitement that sends the heart-rate soaring. Standing in front of me was the young man from the pub, the one I'd 'chosen' within seconds of setting eyes on him for the first time. And it seemed, he'd also 'chosen' me: 'My name's Munem,' he smiled at me and I noticed he had an intriguing accent. 'I've seen you around town a lot,' he said, 'passing my college and at Victoria Hall when Cleo Laine and Johnny Dankworth performed there on Saturday.' So he'd been to the same concerts that I'd been to and I'd never noticed him before today. How was it possible?

But now that we had finally noticed each other, it seemed that he was as determined as I was that we shouldn't let this opportunity pass us by. 'Would you like to go to the cinema with me next week?' He hesitated a moment, 'If that's all right with you, that is.'

'I'd love to!' I was ecstatic at the prospect of actually going out on a date with him. 'I'll see you outside the Odeon on Wednesday evening at six. It's my day off.' And that's how it started. From the moment we met, I felt Munem was so different from the other boys I knew. He seemed so much more mature, solid, dependable and trustworthy. The local lads seemed interested only in two things: how quickly they could get a girl into bed and then brag about it, and how quickly they could get into a fight with other lads. They slavishly followed the fashion trends – especially, the Teddy boy youth culture, supposedly derived from Savile Row tailors after the War launching a range of clothes that mimicked the style of the Edwardians in the early years of the century. The Teddy boy uniform was a long, dark-coloured drape jacket, sometimes with a velvet trim, high-waisted drainpipe trousers, a high-necked loose collar on a white shirt, a narrow tie and floral brocade waistcoat. The look was set off by chunky brogues or crepe-soled shoes – sometimes nicknamed 'brothel creepers' – and carefully-constructed hairstyles were laden with hair grease with a quiff combed back to form the intriguingly titled 'DA' because it resembled a duck's rear-end.

The Teds in London had become notorious after joining in a riot in Notting Hill in 1958, when racist white mobs attacked black people. In Halifax, violence usually only erupted between the different groups of teenagers when they squared up on opposite sides of a dancehall. But Munem seemed a world away from all of that; he was self-assured about himself and his path in life. He seemed so mature for his age and couldn't care less about the latest teenage fashion trends or spending all his money on clothes. He had no interest in just going out with the aim of getting drunk and then starting a fight with everyone. Nor did he seem obsessed with chasing every girl in sight to collect notches on his bed-post. Munem had grown up in such a different culture to the British boys his age. There'd been no such thing as dancehalls when he was a young teenager but, even now that he was living in England, he certainly didn't haunt them. He was determined to work hard and get the highest possible grades on his course in Halifax, where he was studying the requisite A-levels to enter Birmingham University for his degree. I admired him, I found him incredibly attractive and falling in love with this man seemed like the most natural thing in the world.

We were married in the Birmingham registry office on November 8, 1958 with my parents and my friend Sheila present. I wore a simple but pretty outfit – a skirt and blouse with a turquoise coat and hat. We all went to a restaurant later for the wedding breakfast. I loved being married and was overjoyed when I discovered three months later that I was pregnant. Our son Mazin was born on November 20, 1959, though his arrival three weeks prema-ture was a bit of a surprise. I'd been booked in to give birth in Birmingham at the large hospital attached to the univer-sity but I went into labour during a visit to Halifax to see Mum. Mazin arrived in his own time, weighing in at just five pounds and six ounces. He was small but, despite his early arrival, he was a strong, healthy baby, sweet-natured and adorable.

I enjoyed being a mum but after a while I hankered after a little more stimulation and decided I wanted to return to work. Earning extra money wasn't a pressure on me as we had Munem's scholarship, which also covered living expenses, but I wanted to be a bit more active in the outside world. I wanted a change from nursing and was happy just doing part-time jobs, nothing too demanding because I wanted to have lots of energy left over for the time spent with my little boy and my husband, who was incredibly hard-working. Munem was from a large family who had all been brought up to better themselves, and it had been instilled in them that the way to do that was to study hard and get a good education. He knew he was lucky to have the opportunity of an Iraqi government scholarship to get a good education in England and he was not going to squander it. It was very common to find Iraqi students at British universities, often studying engineering or medicine, and there were a number on the course in Birmingham, all of whom we got to know. Some had British wives or girlfriends, some had children, and others didn't. It was a great life, all of us young and enjoying socialising together with parties, dances and films. We were all so full of plans for the future. With the energy and confidence of young adults – especially in the Britain of the late 1950s and early 1960s, with the deprivations of the war years only a distant memory from childhood – it felt as if anything was possible.

Several of our Iraqi friends had already returned to their homeland where, like Munem, they would be bonded to work for the government for fifteen years as a way of paying back the government-sponsored scholarships that were awarded to the very best and brightest of students. It enabled them to get an excellent education at top foreign universities. The only catch was that, if they decided not to return to Iraq, they would have to pay back the cost of their education and for most people that would have been far beyond their means. Even as we'd watched the news of the coup against the same government that had sent him to England, Munem had no doubts about returning: 'If I don't go, my family will have to pay back the money to the government and they just don't have it.' Even with a new government in power, there'd be no change to regulations like that. So there was never any suggestion that we'd stay in England and make our home there together, even when Munem was offered a job by the huge oil company Shell. He knew he had to turn it down.

So here we were, Maz and I, listening to the flight attendant's clear voice declaring, 'We will be landing at Baghdad airport in 30 minutes. Please fasten your seatbelts and extinguish all cigarettes. Make sure your tray tables are up. The temperature is 42 degrees Centigrade in Baghdad and the time of arrival will be 1400 hours. I hope you had a nice journey.' As our plane landed, I knew that Munem would be waiting for us and I hoped that the airport formalities would be over quickly so we could see him without delay. When the aircraft doors opened and the external stairs had been put in position we joined the file of passengers down the aisle of the plane and to the open door. The heat of the afternoon hit us with such ferocity that we had to catch our breath. 'My God!' I gasped to Barbara, 'I've never experienced heat like this.' I looked down at the outfit I was wearing – a green checked summer-weight coat, knee-length green skirt and short-sleeved blouse. It was perfect for the British summer but more like winter-wear in Iraq. I'd carefully planned what I was going to wear on the plane, something comfortable but also smart because I wanted Munem's first glimpse of me in almost a year to be an appreciative one. But, in just a few seconds, I was sweltering. My discomfort in the heat was forgotten when I looked down on to the tarmac shimmering in the heat haze. I saw Munem – like a mirage – standing there looking up at us. An army friend who worked at the airport had arranged for Munem and Barbara's husband to come out to meet us as soon as the plane landed.

Mazin and I raced down the steps into Munem's waiting arms – the long flight, the tiredness, the heat, were all worth that single moment. Mazin was ecstatic at seeing his dad; he'd missed him so much. A year is like an eternity to a three-year-old but he hadn't forgotten his father. During Munem's absence, we always talked about him and Mazin had understood that after a big trip on a big plane he'd be with Daddy again. Now here he was, and all the sad moments of missing each other disappeared in seconds. We walked away together arm in arm. Baghdad airport was only small at that time, nothing like the large international airport that would later be built further away on the outskirts of the city. I now had my first taste of what it was like to look – and feel – like a foreigner. In Britain, when I walked down the street, I looked and felt entirely at home; I *was* at home. But here, many of the women were covered head-to-toe in the traditional black silk *abaya*, the cloak-like shroud that many Iraqi women wore over their head and body when out in public. Some had their faces covered as well so all that was visible were their eyes. Others were in western dress but most in a conservative version of it – long sleeves, and hemlines to the ankle. Some of the men were in suits but others wore the traditional *dishdasheh*, a long white, flowing robe. Some people stared at us as we walked through the terminal building. I realised that I probably did stand out a bit in this small crowd – blonde hair, fair skin and an outfit that was certainly modest but didn't exactly hide my curves or my slim, toned arms and legs.

We took a taxi for the ten-minute drive to the apartment Munem had found for us. As the taxi wove through the traffic, I was enthralled by the hustle and bustle of daily life, the noise of the vehicles, the clamour of people in the busy streets. Almost down every street, I could hear a voice blaring from loud-speakers and wondered what the announcements were or whether it was a special occasion. Munem told me it was one of the seemingly endless recordings of speeches by the President of Iraq, Abdul Karim Qassem. It struck me how absurd this would be in Britain, to be out and about doing your errands to the incessant sound of the disembodied voice of the prime minister. It seemed that it was impossible to escape politics here even if you were just out doing your shopping.

The excitement of finally being here with Munem swept away any nerves that I might otherwise have had about such a big move. Before I left, I'd been so caught up in the excitement of knowing I'd soon see him again and all the busyness of the preparations, that it had never occurred to me to wonder about *exactly* what I was going to encounter when I got to Iraq. Munem had often spoken of his family and of growing up in Iraq, but he'd never really told me what to expect as a western woman. It had been 30 years since the British mandate in Iraq had ended and an independent Iraq had become a member of the League of Nations – the precursor to the UN – so the country barely featured in the British media at all, apart from those dreadful days when young King Faisal was killed. It wasn't as if anyone was really well-informed about Iraq. If anything, it was thought of only in terms of the swashbuckling Arabian Nights films, myths and fairytales, ancient history and biblical stories – the Hanging Gardens of Babylon, the Tower of Babel, the reputed site of the Garden of Eden, Sinbad the Sailor's adventures and *The Thief of Baghdad* films, ancient Mesopotamia and King Nebuchadnezzar. The reality of life there didn't enter my thoughts in the least. I had no preconceived ideas at all beyond a vague notion that I'd happily spend my days sunbathing. Perhaps it was just as well. Iraq seemed to exist on the edge of my consciousness as the place where my husband came from and the place that I would now call home. No more and no less.

Here I was, 25 years old, a young woman from a small town in north-western England, a wife, a mother, embarking on the biggest adventure of my life and I'd be facing it with the love of my life at my side. I had all of the energy and enthusiasm of idealistic, romantic youth. I didn't even feel the slightest twinge of anxiety or fear when faced with the prospect of a new culture, a new language and a new country with a history as old as Time itself. I was like a blank page, all ready for the story of my new life to be written upon it.

2. New Friends

The hypnotic call to prayer echoed from loud-speakers fixed to minarets across Baghdad, as the muezzin summoned the faithful to the mosques. I hadn't yet changed my watch from British time but I didn't need to look at the clock to know it was 6 p.m. – time for sunset evening prayers. Munem had already explained to me about the calls to prayer at the mosques. He said that the branch of Islam to which his family belonged – the Sunni – was the majority group within the religion but only a minority of the Iraqi population, although they had for decades dominated political and economic life here. The Sunnis, Munem told me, observed five prayer times: at sunrise, say 5.30 a.m., then around 12.30 when the sun is high, 3.30 p.m. when the sun is getting lower, 6 p.m. sunset prayers and 8 p.m. Munem wasn't an observant Muslim, he didn't go to the mosque or say daily prayers and we wouldn't be bringing up our children as Muslims. But he was a spiritual person in his own way. The second-largest grouping within Islam, the Shias, are the majority in Iraq.

We were sitting on the balcony of the third-floor apartment that Munem had rented for us in the Mansour district, a nice area that would soon become very posh indeed. It was part of the modern Baghdad, with lots of cafés and shops and boutiques. The view from our balcony was stunning, and Baghdad seemed to stretch far into the distance in every direction. There were some newer buildings in our neighbourhood but I could also see the old parts of Baghdad, with houses and apartments and shops and mosques densely packed together. The boulevards lined with palm trees looked so exotic. Evening was approaching. I'd just woken up from a nap and I was happy to sit there watching this strange new world go by. Munem and I had so much to talk about and my senses were full of these new smells, sounds and sights. I watched as cars, buses, horses and carts all tried to out-manoeuvre each other on the crowded streets. Drivers, pedestrians and shoppers were shouting at each other but whether it was through the heat or their frustration at the traffic or to be heard above the din, I couldn't tell. The sinuous sounds of popular Arabic music rose up from the shops below us.

The aroma of cooked meat and spices also floated on the breeze, from a cart on the street corner where a man sold liver, chicken, lamb and beef on skewers. Just the smell of it made me feel ravenous. Munem went down to the street and bought a few skewers as a snack for us, coming back with *sumoon* or bread, which was freshly-baked from a shop downstairs. Our kitchen was very basic and only had a sink and a few shelves, on which Munem had stacked crockery, cutlery and pots. The cooker was a single-burner paraffin contraption and I wondered how I was going to manage to cook an entire meal on that. But I was able to make some tea and prepared some sandwiches with the meat Munem brought back from the street vendor. I noticed apprecia-tively that he had gone to the trouble of buying groceries and the fridge was well-stocked.

It was soon time for Munem to set off for his night shift at the huge Dora refinery, about 45 minutes' drive away. The car came to pick him up at 9 p.m. so that he could be there for his shift at 10. He gave us both a hug and kisses. 'Make friends with your neighbours and unpack your things while I am at work,' he said. 'It won't be long before I'm back.' The double door made of a rich dark wood with two small windows closed behind him and he was gone. The two windows in the door were intriguing. They had a dual func-tion: for security reasons, they could be opened so you could see who was there before opening the door, and for cultural reasons, the windows safeguarded the modesty of the women, who covered themselves head-to-foot and didn't want to be caught unawares by a man coming to the door unannounced. One of the windows could be opened just a fraction, without having to open the door into a room where the more traditional women might not be wearing their *abaya* or their veils. Many of them only put the *abaya* over the top of their ordinary clothes when they went out or when male visitors came to the house.

I came in from the balcony and took a closer look at our new home. The windowed front door opened into a large entrance hall with the kitchen, bathroom and toilet leading off it. Along a corridor were two bedrooms and a sitting room with a balcony running the whole length, which I liked. It gave the rooms a sense of space and open-ness. The sitting room wasn't large but big enough for four armchairs and a settee that had been re-covered in the brightest imaginable shade of shocking pink – a cast-off from his family's house, I discovered. Our bedroom was bare apart from the double bed and wardrobe and Mazin's room, on the other side of the sitting room, was painted a bright, fresh white making it seem cool and spacious. It was furnished with a single bed, wardrobe and chest of drawers. Tomorrow, I thought, I'll go and meet the neighbours and I'll write to Mum and tell her about every-thing. I slipped into my new bed, thinking of Munem, who'd be working throughout the night, and went off to sleep with the muted sounds of this strange new city in my ears.

The call to prayer that had seemed so exotic and mystical the evening before woke me abruptly at 5.30 a.m. As I stretched myself awake, I luxuriated in the feeling of the sun on my face, already hot despite the early hour. I'd been exhausted and slept deeply. Mazin hadn't stirred so I decided to let him sleep for a bit longer. My clothes were still in the suitcase untouched from the night before; I'd been too tired to unpack then but now I wanted to feel settled, to feel that I belonged here. I began to arrange my clothes next to Munem's and, opening a drawer, I found a stack of letters I'd sent to him over the past nine months.

I was touched to see a photograph of him taken by an army friend. Munem was standing next to his personal locker at the base where he'd done his army training and, pinned prominently on his locker door, I could see a photo of Mazin and me. Munem stood smiling next to it, looking tanned and even more handsome than usual in his uniform. The army training had made him so much fitter and his muscles more defined. I was so happy to see that he'd saved all my letters to be read again and again, reminders of our love and life together, when he missed us. I hoped it had made me and Mazin seem closer to him. It was good to know that he had missed me as much as I had missed him. I opened the letters and read a couple of them. They brought back all the feelings and experiences I'd had after Munem left for Iraq:

July 1961

Dear Munem,
I have just finished packing and clearing out our flat in Birmingham. Mr and Mrs Ora [our landlord and his wife] hope that you arrived in Baghdad safely. Mazin

misses you very much and is unusually quiet with the change of routine. Northfield Road has lost its charm and we will be looking forward to seeing my mum. I finished working in Selly Oak Hospital and so I don't take Mazin to the nursery any more.

Your friend Ramsey came to see me a few times and he also invited me to go and have some lunch with the family he lives with. I have spent three lovely years here and have met a lot of people. So saying goodbye to them all will be a little emotional.

Mr and Mrs Ora got attached to Mazin during these last three years. They still borrow him from time to time and have gone through the baby difficulties with me. At first I thought they wouldn't like having a baby here, but I was wrong. They treated him like the grandchild they should have had, but didn't.

Ramsey will be taking me to the bus station soon and I am handing in the door key ready for my last goodbyes. How I hate them. Tell me about everything – must go –

Love and kisses from me and Mazin – all my love Pauline.

August, 1961

Dear Munem,
I have arrived in Halifax and am staying with my mum. She has moved into a one-bedroom flat. We are sleeping

on a mattress in the sitting room. The view from her window is stunning and looks over the Calder river valley for miles. The fields and hills are interrupted by a few scattered unused mills. We are a stone's throw from Hebden Bridge and the Hebble river runs through it. It is a quaint village.

I got a job in Mackintosh's sweet factory, they wanted staff for the Christmas rush. My cousin Fred and Sylvia, his wife, work there – he is Rita's brother and Aunty Polly's son. Aunty Polly is Mum's elder sister and keeps an eye on her, what with my mum being the youngest. It will be some handy money for the time being. Mum is looking after Mazin and loving every moment.

I have visited all the family and we got to talking about my Grandma Marshall, Mum's mother. She came from Northern Ireland during the potato famine, with my great-grandfather, Patrick, and great-grandmother and her sister and brother. They sailed to Hull, and during the journey caught the flu and later died. The children were left orphans and distributed to different families around England but her brother was sent to Canada. My grandma came to Halifax to live with a family who were in the wholesale business and were shop-keepers. Finally, she married one of the sons, James, my grandfather, who was deaf and communicated with everyone by sign language. The only person he understood was my grandma. I didn't know this until we started talking about the family history. It must have been hard for her.

I hope you are coping well with your army training and will soon qualify as an officer.

Write soon. Mazin sends his love.

All my love,

Pauline.

I carefully folded away the letters and walked into the kitchen, where I put the kettle on. Now, it was time for my wee boy to start his day. Mazin had slept soundly, seemingly unfazed by his new surroundings and his new bed, obviously confident that if Mummy and Daddy were here, all would be well in his little world. 'Mazin, Mazin,' I repeated his name gently. His sleep-filled eyes opened and he smiled and reached out for my hands as I scooped him up in my arms. 'Let's go downstairs to get something for breakfast. You can go in your pyjamas.' He hooked his arm around my shoulder and murmured, 'Okay, Mummy.' We'd spent so much time together while his dad was here in Iraq, and we were very close. I looked down at my sleepy son and thought these were such precious moments. I wanted him to feel settled here and I wanted to make a happy home for him. There'd be adjustments for him to make as well, just like me, but I was certain he'd adapt. The most important thing was that we were all here together now as a family. The time would soon fly and Mazin would be starting school and we'd be spending much of the day apart. So I wanted to make the most of our time together, to really enjoy him before he had to start school.

Living in Baghdad would be an adventure that the two of us would embark on together – and it would start today with breakfast. There was no one on the tiled stairway as we padded down to the street. The shop-keeper was very helpful and I surmised that Munem must have already mentioned to him that I'd be coming in here to buy groceries but that I didn't speak any Arabic just yet beyond a couple of words. I discovered to my great relief that most people seemed to know how to speak even a little English because it was taught at school, and they were always eager to practise the language. The shop-keeper was no exception.

'Give me six eggs please,' I said, pointing to them as well just in case there was any misunderstanding.

'Yes-here-take-please,' the shop-keeper replied in heavily accented but enthusiastic English.

'What do you want, Maz?' My son loved milk so he took a pint of banana-flavoured water-buffalo's milk, which was used widely instead of cow's milk. It didn't have any fat in it at all and tasted like the long-life milk that we had in England.

Laden with our breakfast ingredients – eggs, clotted cream or *gamer*, jam, freshly baked bread and milk – we raced up the stairs seeing who could get up to the top first, panting and laughing when we got there. The kettle was shrieking at us as we opened the door and I set about making breakfast. I perched the teapot on the top of the kettle to keep it warm for when Munem came home from work. I put the eggs into the kettle to boil for a few minutes, then Maz and I went to sit on the balcony to watch the people below while we ate our bread and jam. My son was enthralled by all the hustle and bustle below him. The doorbell rang. I picked up Mazin and, looking through the little window, we saw Munem's smiling face. 'How did you manage?' he asked.

I opened the door and he lifted his son and gave him a big hug and a kiss. Mazin gazed into his father's eyes, loving every moment of the attention that he'd missed so much and flung his little arms around Munem's neck. He held on tight, not wanting to let go of his father. I gave Munem a kiss on the cheek, and felt such longing for him. I too wanted to hold him and not let go. But that could wait for later, when we had the chance to show our love. We had waited so long, so many months, that a little longer wouldn't hurt.

Munem looked tired after his night shift but nonetheless very happy to be with us and have his first proper family breakfast for almost a year.

'We're fine,' I replied. 'I've made breakfast. It's out on the balcony.' We sat down and chatted, just like old times again, but even better. Munem stayed up talking to us and playing with Mazin for as long as he could, but, with another night shift ahead of him, he finally said, 'I'm so tired, I must sleep. Wake me up at 3.30, there's a good girl. Then we'll go to see my family. They can't wait to meet you and Maz. I tried to make it another day but they were too impatient, so I couldn't get out of it. We'll make it a quick visit.' He went off to bed and I cleared away the breakfast things. Mazin and I slipped away quietly, to go and introduce ourselves to our neighbours. There were three other flats on our floor and a flight of stairs going up to the roof where the washing could be hung out to dry. One flat was still unoccupied so we knocked on the second door, and it was answered by a European woman with twin boys, still just toddlers, hanging onto her skirt.

'Hello, my name's Pauline. I moved in yesterday. I live just across the way.'

'Come in, please come in,' she smiled. 'My name's Maria. I'm so glad to have someone I can speak to!' She ushered us into her sitting room, which was bigger and of a slightly different lay-out to ours. It had two large windows to the bedrooms to let the light filter in. These were her sons' bedrooms and I guess it was easier for her to keep an eye on them from the sitting room. 'Now, what would you like to drink?' she offered. 'Tea, cola, coffee?'

'I'd love some tea, please, milk with no sugar and Mazin would love orange juice. How long have you been here?' I asked her.

'It's a year already. I was an au pair in England, where I met my husband. My family sent me there to learn English.

35

It helps to know languages in my family's hotel business back in Switzerland. I can speak German, French and now English. My mother didn't agree about the marriage, so they are upset with me at the moment, but they will come around.' She paused to take a sip of the black sage tea, as her children vied for her attention. We chatted for a while but I could see that she had her hands full with the twins so I said my goodbyes and thanked her for her hospitality.

'Do please come and see me when you have time, Maria,' I said.

Back in our flat, Maz and I poked our head around the bedroom door. Munem was still asleep. We ventured back out into the hallway to see if any of our other neighbours were at home. I knocked on the door just next to ours and a woman opened it. She seemed surprised to see a stranger there with a child.

'I'm Pauline, your neighbour,' I explained. 'I arrived here from England yesterday. I've just come to say hello.'

She was very welcoming. 'Come in! I'm Taleh. My husband, Hashim, works for Iraqi Broadcasting.' Her daughter was playing with a doll and was a little bit older than my son. 'This is Maysoon,' she said, introducing us to her daughter.

'And this is Mazin,' I smiled at my son.

The flat had a lovely aroma of jasmine. It was decorated nicely and I instinctively felt I'd have more in common with Taleh than Maria. Taleh, who I learnt was Turkish, also spoke perfect English.

'I work in the Turkish section at the broadcasting station,' she explained. 'I read the news and tell the listeners a bit about daily life in Iraq.'

'I would love to do something like that,' I said. 'I need something to keep me busy.'

'They can't find anyone for the English section,' said Taleh. 'I'll ask my husband if it would be possible for you to work there.' I couldn't believe my luck: a new friend *and* the prospect of a new job all in the space of a few hours.

By now it was early afternoon and back in the flat, we tip-toed into the bedroom again to see if Munem was still asleep. Mazin was so eager to wake him up. I tickled Munem's feet. 'Time to get up! It's 3.30.' He must have been tired still but he didn't protest at being woken up. I looked down at my handsome husband as he stretched out his long limbs and I could hardly wait to feel his skin next to mine, to feel our bodies entwined after our enforced separation. 'Daddy, I love you!' Mazin flung himself onto his father, planting a kiss on his cheek.

'I love you too, son.' Munem smiled and looked down at that beautiful little face gazing up at him so adoringly. He stroked our child's dark hair, holding him close. In that perfect moment, it was just the three of us, secure in the knowledge that we were loved, we were together and feeling that nothing could ever separate us again.

3. A New Family

The gritty dust churned up by the traffic hung in the heavy air as the taxi careered through Baghdad, taking us past the grand British embassy, a reminder of colonial times when, in the wake of World War One, Iraq had become a territory under British mandate. We went past the Iraqi national broadcasting centre, which Taleh had mentioned to me just that morning, and which would soon become so familiar to me. The taxi sped along the Corniche, the riverside boulevard along the Tigris, the river around which this extraordinary, ancient city had grown. We went on past the many riverside parks where families had picnics and people strolled. Now that I was at street level, I had a close-up view of the shops and restaurants, the apartment buildings and offices that I'd seen from the vantage point of our balcony.

Since arriving in Baghdad less than 24 hours ago, I'd barely had time to even imagine what Munem's family would make of us. Mazin, eager, energetic and the image of his father, would, I felt certain, win their hearts immediately

by virtue of his gender – a precious first-born son – and keep
their love by virtue of his sweetness. But how would they
react to me, the English wife they'd never met before, the
foreigner, the non-Muslim? I could feel that I was drenched
in sweat, from the heat, from the jostling of the journey in
the stuffy taxi and with a nervousness that had begun to
clasp the pit of my stomach. The perspiration ran down my
face, taking my carefully applied make-up with it.

An hour later we were there, in Karradah, a suburb of
Baghdad. The Al-Samarraie family home was an ordinary-
looking single-storey house. Surrounded by high walls and
behind an iron gate, it seemed to me to be almost hiding
away from the prying eyes of the world. The house had an
air of benign neglect, heightened by the sludge-green paint-
work that had long since faded. The garden resembled an
overgrown orchard, with date palms towering above the
orange trees, shading the house from the unforgiving sun.
By now, it was six in the evening and the oppressive heat of
the day had begun to subside. As we got out of the car, the
faint breeze that cooled my face and my bare arms and legs
carried with it the heavy, cloying, unmistakable scent of
gardenias. I took a deep breath – and not just to inhale the
perfumed air. I was as ready as I was ever going to be to
meet my new extended Iraqi family.

A young boy came out to greet us and usher us in – it was
my husband's brother, Assarm, the youngest of his nine
siblings and just three years older than our son. As an only

child, I found it impossible to imagine what it must have been like growing up in such a big family. Munem had five sisters and four brothers. Such a big family was hardly unusual here but I wondered how on earth people managed to make ends meet. Munem's parents had brought up ten children on his father's wage as a local policeman so they certainly weren't wealthy. It must have been a struggle at times but all of the children had received the best that their parents could afford to give them. Having large families and raising them with the support of the extended network of relatives was very important here, whereas in Britain that constant contact between the generations had largely receded. In some Iraqi families there might be three, perhaps four generations living under the same roof. Family ties, kinship and tribal links played a huge role in daily life in Iraq and gave people a very strong sense of loyalty, continuity and belonging.

Munem greeted his young brother warmly and introduced us. 'Hello, Assarm,' I said, reaching out and playfully ruffling the child's hair. My brother-in-law, I mused to myself, is young enough to be my son, and my son now has an uncle not much older than himself. Mazin at least had instantly found a playmate. So far, so good. I braced myself, not knowing quite what I would find in the bosom of Munem's family – immediate and loving acceptance or a viper's nest or something in between. We followed Assarm to the back of the house, where a long, covered verandah ran the length of the lawn. A row of chairs stretched from one end of the verandah to the other; all were occupied by family members and every single one of them was studying me intently. A few neighbours had even turned up to see Mazin and me, the new arrivals from Britain. There were so many people gathered in one place that it felt as if half of Karradah had turned up to inspect us. Munem introduced me to his mother and I gave her a big hug and kissed her on both cheeks. I put aside the usual British reserve about such physical displays of affection with virtual strangers and just went for it. I may not have been very well-travelled but I knew such greetings were usual here, just like in parts of Europe. I also knew instinctively that I had to make a very good impression immediately if I had any chance of winning over this powerful woman, the family matriarch.

As is the Arab custom, my mother-in-law, Bedria, was more commonly addressed using the name of her first-born son – Umm Faleh, mother of Faleh – just as I would come to be known by the family and my Arabic-speaking friends as Umm Mazin, mother of Mazin. My mother-in-law spoke no English so greeted me in Arabic, *'Assalam alaikum.'* This is the universal greeting to fellow Muslims and non-Muslims alike and means 'peace be upon you'. Other greetings are equally gracious and a simple good morning in Arabic when translated into English can mean a graceful 'I wish you a morning of light' or 'A morning of roses to you'. They made English greetings seem so ordinary by comparison.

Now, I was struggling to remember the basic, few words of Arabic that I'd learned from Munem, and offered a cautious '*Shlonich?*' to enquire how she was.

'*Ziena*' – good – she replied, matter-of-factly.

I looked around to see which of the men in the group might be Munem's father.

'He's at work,' Munem said, 'at the police station in Babel Shergi, not far from here.'

As I shook hands with everybody, I felt like a VIP, like one of those foreign dignitaries at a reception, and I was trying desperately to remember everyone's name and being careful to greet each of them equally warmly. Next was Bedri – his name was the masculine equivalent of his mother's. He was a handsome man with the same huge brown eyes and dark hair as Munem, though not as tall. I learned to my great relief that Bedri was a schoolteacher and that English was his subject. His spoken English was very good and that made communicating so much easier. I was especially relieved because I knew that he at least would be able to translate for his mother and father if Munem wasn't with me at other times. I couldn't be sure how long it would take me to learn enough Arabic to be able to communicate with them. Bedri was very welcoming but, even though I'd never seen him before, I was struck by how unwell he looked. His breathing seemed quite laboured. It would have been too impertinent to say anything to him about it at the time but, when I asked Munem about it later, he told me that Bedri had had rheumatic fever as a child and that had left him with a heart-valve defect.

Next in line was Khania, the eldest daughter, who had two young sons. I then met Munem's younger sisters Faleha, Madeha, Hashmia and Emel, who were all at high school. They kissed me and said hello, though one or two seemed a little shy. They spoke to me in cautious English, trying out some of the words they'd learned at school. I was introduced to another of Munem's brothers, Hashim, who was just a little older than Assarm. I noticed that the women of the house were dressed modestly but in a western style, not covered in the all-encompassing *abaya*. As I'd noticed at the airport, many Iraqi women had adopted the western fashions and, as I was soon to discover, there were large numbers of people from all over the world working or studying in Baghdad and elsewhere in Iraq, so it was very common to see people in what I'd consider ordinary clothes of the kind you'd see pretty much anywhere on the streets of Britain. The dress I'd chosen for my introduction to the family was tailored, flattering and snug-fitting, with the hemline at my knee – inspired by Audrey Hepburn's wardrobe in one of my favourite films, *Breakfast at Tiffany's*. The design was the height of fashion at the time, a beautiful 1960s classic but I had a vague feeling that my sense of style may not have been entirely appreciated by my in-laws.

I was grateful to be offered a chair at the table on the verandah, partly because I still felt rather hot and bothered from the taxi journey and partly because I'd begun to feel a little overwhelmed by all these pairs of eyes watching my every move. Aromatic sage tea was poured from the large teapot, which had been brewing on the charcoal fire near the verandah. I held the steaming cup and breathed in the smell of the sage, sipping the hot drink, which was undiluted by the milk I'd normally add to my usual cup of tea. The taste was so different from what I'd been used to at home where one brand of tea leaves was virtually indistinguishable from another. Plates full of delicious home-made pastries were set down on the table in front of us. Munem's mother and sisters had made the cakes especially for our visit and filled them with dates that had been picked from the palm trees in their garden.

The family members who spoke some English were eager to practise on me but inevitably the conversation soon became rather stilted once we got beyond the pleasantries. We'd grown up in very different environments so it was hard to find a lot of common ground in a rather awkward first meeting like this. I struggled to relax, feeling, rightly or wrongly, that everyone was probably casting a somewhat critical eye over me, judging me, my behaviour, my clothes, and my demeanour. I shivered – though by now, I couldn't tell whether it was the evening breeze which was cooling or the atmosphere surrounding me. I knew I was too much my own person to bow down to whatever expectations Munem's family might have of me. I was determined to hold my own with them. And I was determined to keep my identity and not change for anyone. Why should I? In the back of my mind I knew they didn't really want me or my son here; they'd written to Munem telling him as much, telling him to forget me and leave me and our son in England.

An essential part of the mother's role as family matriarch was to choose her sons' wives – and my mother-in-law had not chosen me. I knew that Umm Faleh was not pleased that her son had neither asked her permission nor even informed her before he'd arrived back in Iraq ahead of us. She looked upon me as some foreigner who'd stolen her son. I wondered what my mother would say to that, being far away in England while I was here with my Iraqi husband, who she'd never have accused of 'stealing' me away from her. My mother respected my choice and, loving me as much as she did, she only wanted me to be happy. Tradition here dictated that a family's first-born – in this case, Munem's eldest brother, Faleh – should have been the first to marry. Faleh would, when the time came, be a dutiful son and let his mother choose his wife for him. Unlike Munem, he would abide by her choice of a suitable bride. But Munem had broken their rules and he'd stood up to the family, just as I would later do. The family may not have chosen me but Munem had, and nothing they would ever say or do to me in the future would matter more than that.

I was relieved when Munem finally turned to his mother and said, 'I'm sorry, but we have to go now. I'll have to go to work soon.' Everyone got up from the table and, as Mazin reluctantly left his new playmates to their game, we said our goodbyes to the others. It was a short walk up to a busy street where we found a taxi to take us home. Munem would have just enough time to get ready before he was picked up for his night shift. Later, after I'd put Maz to bed, I stood on the balcony looking out across the night-lights of Baghdad. The air was so much more comfortable now than the steamy day had been and I was at last able to relax and think about the events of the day. It had been an eventful 24 hours – new home, new friend, possibly a new job and a new extended family.

I thought of how my son had played so happily with his two cousins, Khania's sons, and his young Uncle Assarm. It was if he'd known them all his life rather than a matter of minutes. Thank God – or thank Allah as they say here – for the adaptability and resilience of children and their acceptance of what *is* rather than what should be or could be. What happens to us as adults that we lose that ability? I hoped I'd be able to enjoy the same adaptability in immersing myself in life here and that I'd be able to take whatever came and make the best of it. As I thought of my new extended family and of the challenges of this new country, I wondered how easy all that would be.

4. Baghdad's New Correspondent

My neighbour and new-found friend, Taleh, was a woman of her word. At 10 a.m. sharp we'd arranged to go to the Iraqi Broadcasting Centre so she could introduce me to her husband, the manager of the foreign-language sections there. I got ready quietly so as not to disturb Munem who was asleep after his night shift. I chose my outfit carefully. It was another sweltering day and I wanted to feel as comfortable and confident as possible and make a good impression. I put on a sleeveless green top, which had a small, neat collar and a flared floral skirt, cinched at the waist with a brown leather belt; my sandals and handbag co-ordinated with my belt. Now, I felt ready for anything.

I left Mazin playing happily with Taleh's daughter, under the supervision of their maid, and Taleh drove the short distance to work. As Taleh parked her car in a side street, I recognised the building as being the one the taxi had driven past on our way to visit Munem's family the day before. We walked to the front entrance, where security guards were on duty, carefully searching people's bags and other belongings. We gave our handbags to one of the officers and, after a very thorough search, he returned them without a word and motioned to us to continue on our way. I was surprised at the level of security but given that this was the national Iraqi broadcasting company, security measures were expected to be stringent. 'It's like going through airport security,' I remarked to Taleh, as I fumbled to fasten my bag. For her it was an everyday occurrence. She led me to the back of the main building, where the foreign-language section was housed, and where her husband was expecting us.

'This is Mrs Pauline Samarraie, our new next-door neighbour,' said Taleh, by way of introduction.

'Pleased to meet you,' I said, shaking his hand.

'I have heard so much about you and your son Mazin. I feel I already know you so well,' he said, giving me a big smile and shaking my hand so briskly that I wondered if I'd have any fingers left by the time he released them.

'Sit down, sit down.' Hashim was very friendly and enthusiastic. I felt hopeful that Taleh had already given her husband a positive impression of me and that just maybe I had the job in the bag already and this meeting would be a mere formality. 'We already have Mr Kareem, who reads the news,' he explained, 'but we need something new and different and more interesting for our foreign listeners to relate to.'

'What kind of new things would you like to introduce?' I asked, a little mystified about exactly what he was looking for. I'd never done work like this before but I wanted to seem self-assured – though not too over-confident in case he assumed I knew a little more about the job than I actually did.

'I have some money allocated for music and we'd like to hear about the history of Iraq,' he said, leafing through papers that were piled on his desk. He got up and directed me to the studio to meet the head of the English section, who was sitting in the staff lounge, along with people who worked in the Syrian Arabic, French, Urdu and German sections.

'This is Mrs Samarraie, our new member of the English section,' he said. They all smiled and seemed friendly enough. 'I'm sorry, Pauline, I have to go now. I have an appointment and I will be late. Please make yourself comfortable and get acquainted with the rest of the staff until my wife comes back.' And that was my successful job interview, I mused to myself. I'd just become the newest employee of the foreign section of Iraqi radio.

Taleh took me to meet the senior executive in charge of the network. We drank strong black, sweet tea chased down with a glass of water, which was very welcome at this point. I had found it a bit exhausting, shaking hands with a roomful of strangers, and smiling constantly and making small talk. I was probably a bit jet-lagged as well and certainly not yet used to the heat that was sapping more of my energy with every minute. I just wanted to go home and rest.

'Come on, Pauline, let's go,' Taleh said, giving me a nudge, as if she'd been reading my mind. Glad to be going, I got up, shook hands again with everyone and we said goodbye.

When I got home I found Munem awake and eager to hear about my morning.

'How did everything go?'

'Fine, fine, I got the job.'

'I'm so happy for you,' he said, giving me a big hug. 'I've finished my night duty for this week, so we can go out and celebrate, just you, me and Mazin.' And it was indeed a night of celebrations.

In the coming months, I had no doubts that I'd made the right decision. I made a big effort to feel as if I belonged here. Not long after I arrived, Munem and I underwent a simple civil marriage ceremony in accordance with Iraqi law. And I tackled my new career with gusto. I really looked forward to going into work. Back home in England, I'd never have imagined working in broadcasting or anything to do with the media. It was all so different from what I'd done in the past, my years of nursing and, later, the less challenging part-time jobs I'd taken when Mazin was a baby. But here, I was willing to try anything and just see what happened. I looked at the format of the existing programmes and tried to find ways to make the slots I'd have fun and interesting. There was a regular presenter who read the news bulletins. They always sounded so much the same to me and so pedestrian that it barely mattered which day or time you listened. It only ever seemed to be 'President Abdul Karim Qassem went to... the President said... the President did...' The news was translated into English by the Iraqi news agency and always had to be read in full detail. Frankly, it was pretty boring and so carefully monitored and structured that there was never anything contentious or challenging. I'd occasionally fill in if the newsreader was away but my main job was to present a feature called *What the Papers Say,* a daily review of the Iraqi newspapers. I didn't think they were any more informative than the news bulletins, thanks to the censorship of the Iraqi news agency which also provided the translations for us, but it was good to build up experience of being in a studio and to gain the skills of a radio presenter.

I realised immediately that, if I was this bored with the predictability of these programmes, many of our listeners would also be and might just choose to listen to other broadcasters. I thought we needed something lively to keep them interested and attract new listeners to our shortwave transmissions that were heard abroad. So I visited the National Museum in Baghdad, which was considered to be among the most important museums in the world, thanks to its treasures. They ranged through several millennia from the Stone Age to the present day and visiting the museum was like having another world open up to me. Little by little I introduced items about history and culture, along with eastern and western music into the programming. The listeners seemed to love the new, more creative approach. Letters came in from all over Europe. I was receiving so many that I decided to make a feature of them and launched *Post Bag Corner*, in which I'd read out many of the letters and cards. I discovered that this often encouraged even more people to both listen and write in, just to see if their letters would be featured.

It was entirely up to me what I wanted to do with my programmes and, as I got to know more people in Baghdad, I started to include some of them in my features. I'd invite my British ex-pat friends to come into the studio and I'd ask them about their lives and their work, their impressions of Iraq and their thoughts about home. I'd go to hospitals and other places where ex-pats worked and interview them there about their roles and their background and their hopes for the future. I settled quickly into a comfortable and well-ordered daily routine: I worked most days, so I enrolled Mazin in a good private pre-school, where he was taught English and Arabic. He was a very sociable little boy and loved having the company of other children. My own social circle was broadening all the time too, as friends we'd met in Birmingham gradually returned to Iraq after completing their studies. I felt so happy that I had found a job that was so stimulating and interesting. I had a free hand to do whatever I liked; no one had bothered much before, so anything I did was going to be an improvement. It was nerve-wracking and challenging at times but I just grabbed the opportunity and thought I'd give it a go. That was my attitude to life in general, not just my job. I'd worked since I was a teenager and saw no reason to stop now that I was a married woman and a mother. I loved being both but I did want a bit of life for myself, something that would stretch me and get me out into the wider world.

When I had time off and when Munem wasn't working, the three of us would explore Iraq. We visited Samarra, about 60 miles from Baghdad – Munem's family's home-town, from where they took their name. I climbed the spiral minaret, which is one of Iraq's most famous tourist attractions. The Malwiya tower, which rises more than 160 feet, was built by Caliph al-Mutawakil in the ninth century. Iraq, I was discovering, was an amazing country. I'd thought England had an extraordinary history but Iraq seemed to go so far back into antiquity. There were the Sumerians, who came from Iran and northern Anatolia in the fourth millennium BC and founded a culture that was credited with pioneering developments in cuneiform writing, mathematics and political institutions, the arts and theology. There were the many other pre-Islamic kingdoms of ancient Mesopotamia, 'the land between the rivers', as the Greeks called it, referring to the Tigris and Euphrates. Alexander the Great had swept through here, as had the Tartar hordes of Tamurlane, the Persians and the Ottoman Turks. The Abbasid caliphs – Arab Muslims who claimed descent from an uncle of the Prophet Mohammed – had made Baghdad the political, cultural and economic heart of the Islamic world in the Middle Ages. Most of these cultures had left their mark in some way. It was no exaggeration to call this land the cradle of civilisation and for many, many centuries its strategic importance had centred on its location on the overland route between Europe and Asia, the rich land that lay in the Fertile Crescent between the two great rivers, and much later, the extraordinary oil reserves that would be discovered below that land.

The more I read about Iraq and the more I saw of it, the more I became entranced by the wonders of this country. I saw the Arch of Ctesiphon – *taq-i-kisra* in Arabic – one of the treasures of Iraq. The arch was built by the Parthian Persians in 400AD and is the largest single-span vault of unreinforced brickwork in the world. It rises about 110 feet, with a span of about 75 feet, and is part of the ruins of a palace built on the banks of the Tigris, south of Baghdad. Munem enjoyed our trips too but, whereas I wanted to see the remnants of ancient Iraq, he had a special love for the new, modern, industrialised Iraq. He looked forward to seeing how the oil industry was developing because there'd been a lot of changes during his time in England. He was especially interested in seeing Kirkuk, the oil centre of northern Iraq, and the huge refinery there. Kirkuk was also home to the tomb of the Old Testament prophet Daniel.

'A penny for your thoughts,' Munem said to me, taking his eyes off the road for a moment on one of our trips.

'I was just thinking about life and where it takes us,' I replied, smiling over at him.

'You think too much,' he said, covering my hand with his. 'I've decided we're going to have a New Year's party, and I have invited all our friends.' What a wonderful way to see in the New Year. The party was fabulous; the flat was packed with people. I stood on the balcony alone for a moment with the celebrations noisily under way behind me and in the first moments of the New Year I thought of my mother back in England. I wanted her to be here, sharing my life, enjoying our success, watching my son grow in confidence and ability day by day. My New Year's resolution was to write to her and ask her to come to visit us this year. But it seemed as if the year had barely started when Iraq was again plunged into political turmoil.

Five years earlier, I'd been in my Birmingham living room, watching the television pictures of the King being ousted in the coup that took his life and ended the monarchy in Iraq forever. Now it was so much closer to home and it was all unfolding here in Baghdad. In early February 1963, the commander of the air force, Brigadier Jalal al-Awqati, was assassinated and dissident military officers who were members of the newly-formed socialist Baath party, along with other Arab nationalists, attacked an important military base. As forces loyal to the plotters headed for Baghdad, news of the coup attempt was broadcast to the country.

My boss told us all that it would be safer if we took a few days off because the security situation was too volatile to be at work. During this time, I visited a friend from the Birmingham days, Ramsey, who'd recently finished his doctorate in civil engineering and returned to Baghdad. His family lived just down the road from our flat. While I was there, we heard the roar of planes above the building and rushed up to the roof terrace to see what was happening. It was like watching a war film: in the skies above us, a plane was trying desperately to avoid the fire from another, diving in this direction and that to try to escape being hit. I watched in amazement, hardly believing that it was real life and not just some stunt at an air show. But Ramsey didn't seem at all disturbed by it and I found some solace and reassurance in his measured reaction. If he wasn't panicking, why should I? When it had all finished we went inside just as if we'd been watching some aerial display and the show was now over.

In the streets of Baghdad, members of the communist party were mobilised and they took to the streets in support of the government. They rallied outside the Defence Ministry, where the President, Abdul Karim Qassem, and his senior officials had set up a command centre. Fierce fighting broke out but the government's supporters and the troops that had remained loyal to the President were no match for the well-organised, well-trained military units that besieged the building. The rebel forces quickly overcame the resistance and stormed the Defence Ministry, capturing the President and several of his officials. The outcome was swift; they were brought before a tribunal, sentenced to death and executed by firing squad. The President's bullet-ridden body was later displayed on Iraqi television to prove that he had been killed. It was extraordinary for me to see a political system that acted so swiftly, and it seemed at the time, so harshly. But these were the political realities and Iraqis seemed to accept them without question. When the coup was over and the new government installed under President Abdul Salem Aref, we were told the national security situation was stable enough for us all to return to work at the radio station. But when Taleh and I did get back into the building, I was told that I would no longer be able to broadcast from my usual studio.

Technical problems happened every now and then and studios were taken out of commission until they were repaired but when I walked through my studio, I could see exactly why I would not be broadcasting from there. I was astonished to realise that the same studio, where I'd sat for so many hours, happily playing music, chatting to my studio guests and discussing Baghdad's social life or Iraq's rich culture and traditions, had been transformed into an executioner's chamber: the walls and floors were smeared with dried blood. Machine-gun bullet holes marked the trail of blood all along the length of the wall. Nothing in my life could have prepared me for something like this. As a nurse, of course, I'd been no stranger to the sight of blood – but this was very different: this was a form of brutality that I could not understand. This was deliberate blood-letting. I never found out who was killed there and, under the current climate and the new regime, no one dared to ask, though we could all imagine the terror that those men must have felt as they knew the end had come.

At the time, it was dangerous to express any political opinions or ask any awkward questions about what had gone on, so I resolved to keep my opinions and questions to myself. But I simply could not understand why people have to be killed solely for their political beliefs. Why are thoughts considered so dangerous that one must be killed for them? It had shaken me to see the bloody evidence of the coup in the very studio where I'd been working until so recently. But it was essential that I regain my composure and I knew I couldn't betray even a flicker of emotion to the listeners. I simply announced that there had been a change of government and the republic of Iraq had a new president.

While I had decided to carry on regardless, Taleh eventually found it impossible to do the same. She felt too unsettled and didn't want to stay in Iraq any longer. She returned to Turkey with her young daughter. I heard later that she had started her own business and was doing very well. I was happy for her; she deserved happiness and success. Her husband stayed in Iraq and they divorced. He later married a cousin, a wife who, I'm sure, was seen by his family as being more suitable. I missed Taleh a great deal and thought of her often and appreciated the kindness she'd shown me from that first day, both as a neighbour and a friend. I wouldn't have had this job if it hadn't been for her. And now she'd decided that she could no longer bear to live in Iraq. It was to be the first painful farewell of so many in the years to come.

5. A Visit from Saddam

Iraqis soon got used to having another government that had taken power by force. What was happening on the political scene seemed so removed from my everyday life. I just didn't feel affected by it and, mostly, people simply got on with their own lives and let the politicians fight it out between them. I was more concerned about the upheaval in my home life, after Munem came home from work one day and said he had some news for me. If I'd been expecting an announcement of a promotion or a pay rise, I was mistaken. 'We have to go to live in Dora, in a house next to the refinery.' As if anticipating my resistance, he said quickly, 'It's a three-bedroom house, with a garden and a communal swimming pool.'

I tried to argue: I was happy where I was, we had so many friends around us and Mazin was content in his nursery school. We lived so close to my work now but Dora was about half an hour's drive from the station, so I'd have to take a bus along the rough and bumpy road into

Baghdad. I could see no reason to move out to Dora, when Munem was already being driven back and forth to work there anyway. He tried to reassure me – 'You'll meet other new friends in Dora and still see the old ones, maybe more so now that there's a pool there for our friends to swim in when they come to visit. And there is still your job.' I knew I had no say in the matter and that ultimately it was useless to argue.

Munem's mother came to visit the day before the move. But she didn't kiss me or greet me with any warmth and made no move to help me with the packing. Instead, she inspected the flat like an army sergeant-major, looking over the few basics that we had. I interrupted my packing to prepare a meal while she hovered around and at one point, she even made a big gesture of lifting the pan lid to peer inside and see what I was cooking and whether it was acceptable to her. I learned later that she'd only come because she wanted her chairs back. She was welcome to the lumpy, uncomfortable things – every time I sank into those unwelcoming chairs, they had reminded me of her equally unwelcoming presence! I remembered the first time she'd come to visit the apartment. She'd picked up and had a good look at my possessions, opened the fridge and peered inside and taken the lids off the cooking pots. Her behaviour hadn't changed at all in the intervening time.

To me, she seemed like a difficult, nosy woman and there was a gulf between us right from the start. We simply did not understand each other and it was not just about language and culture, though those differences didn't help. You can overcome them if you really try but initially, I think, neither of us felt overly inclined to try. Mostly, I just accepted her quirks and tried to laugh them off where I could – like the time she asked me to thread a needle for her, not long after I got to Iraq. I thought it was just because she couldn't see clearly enough to do it herself but Munem just laughed and said that the mothers-in-law often do that with their sons' wives, to test whether their eyesight is good enough. It seemed ridiculous. What was she going to do if I failed to thread the needle? Tell Munem to divorce me?

Not even my mother-in-law's silly little tests were enough to get me down because I was more preoccupied with settling into our new house. It had been built by the American contractors who'd built the big refinery at Dora and it had echoes of the American modernist architectural style, with its open-plan reception room, which was both dining room and living room. There was a large garden which was perfect for Mazin to run around in and play with his friends when they came to visit. The front entrance was covered in trailing, sweet-smelling jasmine that created a lovely ambience from the moment you approached the door. The workers' houses were set back behind security gates and were so well guarded that even our visitors had a problem getting in to see us at times. There were a few foreign wives there from Britain, the

United States and the Netherlands but I didn't see a great deal of them because, unlike them, I had a job. I solved the problem of child-care for Maz in a number of ways – Faleha, one of Munem's younger sisters, was still at high school and she'd come and spend her summer holidays with us and look after him. Other times I took him with me or he stayed with Munem's family.

I had to admit that Munem was right about our social life, though; it didn't suffer at all after the move to Dora. We were never short of places to go – friends' houses, parties at the British and American embassies in Baghdad. Our favourite nightclub was one of the many on the banks of the Tigris. The German big-band leader, James Last, whose music was so popular at the time, would often perform there. We were a cosmopolitan group in the Swinging Sixties and we loved the social life. The ex-pat scene centred on westerners and the growing middle class of Iraqi professionals, many of whom had studied abroad – very liberal, nightclubs and dances, a lot of drink, open-air cinema evenings, where we'd all sit at tables outdoors, eating dinner and watching American and British films. The British ones were my favourites because they reminded me so much of home – the quaint villages, the red double-decker buses, the black London taxis, the green and pleasant land where the changing of the seasons was so marked, unlike in Iraq, where it felt like perpetual summer most of the time. In Iraq, the weather was never a factor if we were deciding to do something outdoors. It only seemed to rain on a handful of occasions each year so if we went to an open-air film screening, we could guarantee that we wouldn't be caught in a downpour.

The Engineers' Union held a dance every Thursday night, the last day of the working week ahead of the Muslim holy day on Friday. There were local swimming pools all over Baghdad but we spent a lot of time socialising at poolside parties held at the embassies, the up-market workers' residential developments like our own and at the Engineers' Union and the Ministry of Oil. It was on those occasions that I could be my fun-loving, relaxed self. But it did feel a little schizophrenic at times. In the more conservative and traditional Arab atmosphere and gatherings, alcohol and partying were frowned on and I was supposed to fall into line with convention especially around Munem's family because their expectations of my behaviour were so different from the kind of person I actually was and that I enjoyed being.

This all came to a head in the unbearably hot summer of 1964. Munem completed his work at Dora and he was told that his next assignment would be at the Khanaqin refinery in northern Iraq. It was only a short-term project so it didn't make sense to pack everything and move as a family, which would also have meant I would have to give up my job. I'd have felt quite isolated – there was nothing at Khanaqin but the refinery and the workers' housing complex. So it was decided that Mazin and I would go to live with Munem's family while he was working away. I wasn't looking forward to it. The family, primarily my mother-in-law and her daughters, seemed to find fault with everything I did. I didn't conform to their expectations and they made no allowances for me or acknowledged the efforts I was making to fit in as an English woman who'd made a lot of compromises to come here and create a life with Munem.

During my stay with the family, I came home from work one day and went into my bedroom to change my clothes. The first thing I noticed was that the mirror on the wardrobe door had been smashed to smithereens.

'Who broke the wardrobe mirror?' I asked, in amazement. An accidental breakage is one thing but this had very clearly been done deliberately.

'I did it,' said Munem's younger brother, Bedri, defiantly. He'd apparently been angry at me for putting on my make-up to go out to see friends and to go to work. I had no idea how outraged he'd been that I'd seemed to him to be ignoring his advice about how a western woman should dress and behave in the Arab world. He'd seen me as being obstinate, ignoring his words and rebelling against his wishes. And I suppose I had been, but it had never occurred to me that Bedri had taken it upon himself to try to police such things, when he was only my brother-in-law.

My own husband never tried to make me stop wearing make-up or trying to look presentable, so why on earth should my brother-in-law take it upon himself to do so? It seemed that Bedri felt responsible for me while Munem was working away. His frustration had finally erupted in breaking that mirror. Bedri was always the disciplinarian with his own family, trying to organise the lives of his younger brothers and sisters and the children of his eldest sister. I realised quite soon that nothing I did would ever be good enough, so what was the use of trying?

Munem returned from the north and took up a job with the Gas Administration in Baghdad. Soon after, he came home one day and had some fantastic news: 'We'll be going to France this summer for a couple of months. You, me and Maz. How does that strike you?' I was overjoyed – it would mean the chance to go to England as well and see Mum again, while Munem carried on with the development project he'd be working on. I knew he'd become concerned about how much weight I'd lost and the low-level nagging unhappiness I'd been feeling. I put my weight loss down to the heat and getting lots of exercise, like swimming most days, but there was no denying that I had felt stressed by my relationship with his family and that too was wearing me down physically. Munem thought it would give me a boost to have a break away and he was right; it was just the tonic I needed.

In no time at all it seemed, I was sitting on an Iraqi Airways flight for the second time in two years but now my husband was by my side. The excitement I'd felt that first time, on my way to Baghdad, was a little different – this time, I'd had two years of life there with my husband and our son. Very soon, I'd be able to share all of those experiences with Mum. Two years ago, neither my friend Barbara nor I had known what we'd be going to. Now we did. I hardly saw her any longer; she and her husband and little girl had gone to live in Basra in southern Iraq, where he worked for British Petroleum. I envied her stable life with its structure and routine – her husband came home from work at the same time every day and didn't have to travel or work away. My life had been so busy in these past two years, with moving house twice, at times backwards and forwards living with Munem's family and trying to juggle working with being a wife and mother. All those stresses and strains were forgotten as soon as the plane touched down in Paris. Our home for the next two months was a nice hotel near the beautiful Gothic cathedral of Notre Dame. There were parks close by where Mazin would play; the Metro was just down the road and much easier to use than the London Underground. I'd never been to France before and I marvelled at the beauty of the architecture, the tree-lined boulevards, the ornate statues everywhere and the thriving artistic and cultural life.

Munem was working all day and it was a pity we couldn't really enjoy the famed romanticism of Paris together. But Mazin and I explored the city though I found it difficult at times with an energetic four-and-a-half year-old who understandably had no interest in art galleries or historic buildings. So we spent almost every day in the park where there was so much for him to do and he could race around and burn up all that energy. I struggled with the language and lost confidence in even the few words I'd been able to learn, when I was confronted by waiters or people in shops who clearly expected me to speak perfect French and were very impatient with me when I couldn't. I went to the same cafeteria every day in the hope that they would eventually understand me. A couple of weeks into our stay a telegram arrived, saying that Munem's brother, Bedri – who was in hospital in west London having treatment for his long-standing health problems – had taken a turn for the worse. We were advised to leave for London immediately. We got there as quickly as we could but it was too late. Bedri had died during emergency surgery; the doctors could do nothing to save him. He was so young, just 25 years old.

My sadness was two-fold: for my husband's grief but also, in a sense, for my own remembered loss when my father had died some years earlier when I was just four months' pregnant with Mazin. I thought of Bedri's attempts to try to be strong for his family and keep some semblance of order; I could still see his face when we'd argued over the broken wardrobe mirror and how my behaviour angered him at times, neither one of us really understanding the other. He was a good man and had basically just been trying to do what he thought was right and proper. We made the arrangements for his sealed coffin to be flown back to Baghdad. Munem was grief-stricken to see his young brother's coffin being lifted onto the plane for its lonely journey back to Baghdad, where the family would be waiting and the traditional mourning process would begin. With our sad farewell to Bedri, Munem and I went our separate ways – he went back to France and his work, and Maz and I caught the train to Halifax to stay with Mum. She didn't have a phone at home so I'd just hoped that the postcard I'd sent her from France, letting her know we'd be coming, had arrived in time. Keeping in touch over long distances wasn't so easy back then and we had to rely on letters and telegrams. It was good to see the familiar green countryside, the towns and villages, as the train made its way north from London, and even better to finally arrive in Halifax several hours later.

We bundled into a taxi. 'Rochdale Road, please,' I said, still a little nervous that my postcard may have got lost or not arrived yet and that Mum might not be at home. But within minutes, Maz was running up the three flights of stairs to my mother's one-bedroom council flat. I'd barely had time to knock when the door opened and there she was, looking wonderful and so happy to see us. We hugged, and just the smell of her favourite perfume, *Californian Poppy*, brought such a rush of love for her welling up inside me. I realised how much I'd missed seeing her these past two years and what a huge gap there'd been in my life without any regular contact with her. I'd missed her smile and seeing her so elegantly turned out, just like today – subtle make-up, short blonde curly hair always immaculate, the pretty ear-rings, necklace and brooch that all co-ordinated, all of those extra little touches that showed she'd made an effort.

We had a precious month together to catch up on an entire two years. I wanted her to feel as if she was a part of my life in Iraq so I'd brought lots of photos to show her – our first flat in Mansour and the view from the balcony, the Dora house and the neighbourhood, explaining who was who at parties, photos of us with Munem's family, going swimming and Maz playing with his little friends and cousins. As I saw her delight in going through the photos, I felt sure she'd want to come and see all of these places and people for herself: 'Mum, I wish you'd come and visit me in Iraq. I know you'd like it there.'

The smile left her face and she looked rather downcast. 'Dear, I just can't,' she replied.

'But why on earth not, Mum?'

She looked up at me. 'Because I'm too scared to fly!' My heart went out to her but I'd once been a small-town girl just like Mum. I'd never been on a plane before or even to an airport until I left for Iraq. But I'd overcome any anxiety about it and I hoped I'd be able to convince her that she could as well. I loved her dearly and wanted her to have a good life, a happy life. But I could also see that she had her own little world here and it was probably all she'd ever wanted. She lived in her own little cocoon, afraid perhaps to change or branch out of the same town, the same routines, the same pattern of home, work, telly, where even the characters on her favourite programme, *Coronation Street,* had barely changed. Or perhaps she was simply happy with her lot, happy in what now seemed to me to be a time warp. I'd noticed that since my father died she'd become more reclusive and hesitant about travelling anywhere – especially somewhere as far away and foreign-seeming as Iraq.

So I let the matter drop for now, not wanting to nag about it. There'd be plenty of time to talk her into it. For now, I was just happy to be with her and catch up with family and old friends. My cousins Sheila and Beryl came to visit and we talked about Beryl's plans to emigrate to Canada, where their sister Joyce had already settled. They were more like me in wanting to see something of the world and I understood well enough how hard it was to leave behind your family. But I felt they were lucky because their mother, Amy – my Mum's sister – was more adventurous than my mother so she was likely to visit them in their new home. I met up with old school friends but we just didn't have that much in common any more. They were living very different lives to mine, less varied, and they showed little interest in travelling or living abroad or even really hearing about my life in Iraq. Having seen another culture, I appreciated my own upbringing and my background so much more and I realised how lucky I'd been to grow up where and when I did. I even began to see my home town in a different light. Halifax had developed as a cloth-making town in the Middle Ages and I could see it had a lot of charm that I hadn't always noticed when I lived here. Walking around Halifax this time, meeting up with friends and talking about old times, made me see more clearly than ever how important those formative years had been.

When I did see friends, we usually reminisced most about the past – that was what we had in common, rather than our present lives. We'd talk about our childhood during the Second World War. The War was still two years away from ending when I started school at the age of six in 1943. Like many children, I cried on my first day, when I realised that Mum was leaving me to my fate at Keighley Road Infant and Junior School. But again, like many children, the tears soon dried and the anxiety and fear were forgotten when I looked around the big classroom and saw the beautiful doll's house, the walls covered in pictures, the shelves crammed with books, the containers full of crayons and the vase of flowers that brightened up even the dullest of grey days. But the best thing about our school was the swimming-pool. It was here that we all learned to swim and I discovered that I had an aptitude for sports. When I was 10 I contracted scarlet fever and had to be put into an isolation ward; my best friend, Sheila, got diphtheria at the same time and she was in a hospital nearby. We missed a lot of school that year and as a result, didn't do well in our eleven-plus exams, but we were happy enough to go off to Overnden Secondary Modern school together.

High-school sports days were held in the large field at the back of the school. We all ate in the large canteen, where school dinners consisting of meat, three vegetables and a pudding cost parents two shillings and sixpence a week. One afternoon a week we did sewing and I remember being proud of my handiwork – a blue dressing-gown, a yellow circular skirt and white tennis shorts. I was thrilled to have been made house captain in Madame Cadel House and later, in my final year, to be elected school captain. I turned down the honour because by then we'd moved to the other end of town to be nearer my dad's work, and the trip to school and back each day on two buses was arduous enough without taking on extra responsibilities as school captain. So I agreed to become vice school captain instead. At the end-of-year concert in my final year, I sang a Nat King Cole song – 'Unforgettable' – it was both beautiful and appropriate. Those years had indeed been unforgettable and had given me a strong foundation in life, I felt.

My family was not wealthy – my father worked hard as a foreman for a local engineering works that made bathroom fittings and pipes. During the War he had been a night watchman. He hadn't been able to serve in the military because of a heart problem but he took his duties very seriously. Dad built an air-raid shelter in our back garden and we'd take our next-door neighbour, Lilian, and her elderly mother into the shelter with us. We'd settle in under the corrugated-iron roof until the all-clear sounded. I often thought that my fear of the dark came from those nights crammed underground, wondering what was going on in the skies and streets above us. But most of the time, the War seemed a distant event to me, far away from my life at home with my doting parents, my cousins and my friends. I only remember one bomb dropping on Halifax and, thankfully, no one was hurt. We lived in a council estate, one of seven designed so that they all had their own communal square in the centre. I liked ours best because it had a huge oak tree in the middle.

I thought of my school days as I watched Mazin play happily with his grandmother; he'd be at school himself before too long and had all of those adventures and mishaps ahead of him. Looking back, they seemed such carefree days – why do we never realise it at the time? My life had moved far beyond Halifax now and it would soon be time to return to that life in Iraq. Munem finished his work in France and spent a week with us in Halifax. He and my mother got on very well and she enjoyed seeing him; it was a much warmer relationship than I had with my mother-in-law. Mum always liked the fact that Munem was so polite and well-mannered; he'd been brought up to have respect for people of our parents' generation and it was obvious in the kindliness he showed towards my mother.

Munem asked me to go shopping for his mother and sisters to buy them the sombre, simple black clothes they'd need for the long traditional period of mourning for Bedri. It was a gloomy task but it had to be done. My time with Mum drew to a close. I tried again to persuade her to come back to Baghdad with us but, once more, she refused and I knew better than to keep insisting. She was a gentle, reserved woman but like me, with a strong will of her own. We shed a few tears but I felt certain there'd be many more opportunities to come back and see her.

Besides, Munem, Maz and I were about to make another move, on our return to Baghdad, to an apartment in the Athamiya suburb of Baghdad and I was looking forward to settling in there. But, as soon as we arrived back, we went to Munem's family home, where we spent the next week. We'd missed the first three days and nights of intense mourning for *marhoom* Bedri – the late Bedri – during which the men go to the mosque to pray and the women mourners converge on the family home. His body had been taken to the family's home town of Samarra and, in accordance with Muslim tradition, he had been buried as soon as possible. In Iraq, the process of mourning is often far more expressive than the much more reserved British way. The wailing and keening are seen as therapeutic for those who are grieving, and respectful to the one who has passed away. But I was used to a far more private, silent grief. Where I'd been brought up, if there was a bereavement, the curtains would be closed and people shed their tears privately rather than loudly and publicly. I felt uncomfortable with the family's expectation that I too should be wailing and weeping like the other women, who almost seemed to languish in their sorrow. I too grieved for Bedri but in my own quiet way, something, it seemed to me, they almost wilfully misunderstood as uncaring and hard-hearted.

There was still a constant stream of people coming to the house to pay their respects and among them were close friends of my brother-in-law. I recognised one who'd been to the house on other occasions to see Faleh, one of Munem's other brothers. Faleh and this friend had known each other for years; they often went out to clubs or sat at home and played cards. I gathered that this friend of Faleh's was considered by some to be a bit of a hero because, some years earlier, he'd been among the group of Baathists that had tried to assassinate the leader of the 1958 coup, Abdul Karim Qassem, a year after Qassem had taken power. The President's motorcade had come under fire as it drove through Baghdad but the assassination plot failed and he survived, although with gunshot wounds.

In the hail of gunfire, Faleh's friend was apparently also shot. There were various tales of how he'd managed to get away despite a serious leg wound and how he'd had to extract the bullet himself in order to survive. It was also said that he made a daring escape, hiding out with nomadic Bedouin tribespeople en route to Syria, where this young man – then barely into his twenties at the time – met up with senior Baathists, including one of the founders of the party, Michel Afleq, who welcomed him into the fold as a full member. Faleh's friend later went on to Egypt, where he studied at Cairo university before returning eventually to Iraq.

Whether or not the stories of his daring escape were true, there was no doubt that this was a man who really stood out in a crowd. He was tall, well-built and handsome. There was something very masculine about him but not in an off-putting overtly macho kind of way, more a strong, self-assured phys- ical presence that must have drawn women to him like a magnet. He moved among the other male mourners in the house, engaging in quiet conversation with some, greeting others and exchanging pleasantries, swapping stories and memories of Bedri. His name was Saddam Hussein.

The next time I saw Saddam, he was with President Aref, who was visiting the broadcasting centre. Faleh's friend had apparently been made a member of the President's staff. These were the early days of his steps along the corridors of power.

Within months, there was more political upheaval. The first Arab nationalist Baath party government had been undermined almost from the start by factional in-fighting and disagreements. In November, President Aref and his supporters in the military – including some Baathists – removed the government from power and reasserted their control. Large numbers of Baathist supporters, their sympathisers and others were rounded up and imprisoned. Faleh and his friend, Saddam, were among them. Both were later released but none of us could ever have foreseen the transformation in the fortunes of Faleh's old friend.

6. A Husband's Betrayal

I began to long for something more in our lives. In July, 1965, my wish came true when I discovered that I was pregnant again. Mazin was delighted at the prospect of a little brother or sister. I didn't want him to be an only child, as I'd been. He had his cousins and his younger uncles and his own little friends but I wanted him to know what it was like to have a sibling to share his life, along with us. Unfortunately, Mazin's excitement and my own happiness weren't matched by Munem's reaction. He seemed immersed in work and, while I was certain he was happy about the prospect of becoming a father again, the news barely seemed to register with him. He was always busy, always working, and on the few occasions when he was around, he'd want to socialise with his colleagues or invite them over to see us. I thought — and fervently hoped — that having another child would bring us closer again.

I'd already finished work at the radio station. After two years there, I was no longer enjoying it in the way that I had in my early days. My life was full enough as it was and I was always busy with Mazin and Munem and our social life. Now I had the new baby to look forward to. I was determined to enjoy my pregnancy and make the most of this time. I'd calculated that my baby would probably be due on April 1 the following year. I knew I'd be even busier with the arrival of a second child and that the to-ings and fro-ings of everyday life would be a lot easier if I learned to drive.

Munem had bought an old Fiat, painted green and cream, but he was far too busy with work to teach me to drive so his brother, Faleh, agreed to give me a few lessons when he was home on leave from the army. It was kind of him and I needed his calm presence in the car with me when I braved the Baghdad traffic: 'chaos' is too mild a word for the mayhem of all kinds of vehicles jostling for position in all directions, with carts drawn by horses or donkeys also being manoeuvred through the streets. People seemed to observe only two driving speeds – very fast or very slow. It would be a brave woman who could hold her own among them. Initially, my hands used to shake every time I got behind the wheel but I would just steel myself, knowing that I had a lot to gain by just breaking through that nervousness.

I had a blessed pregnancy – I felt very healthy and fit and I stayed very active, with lots of swimming. The day I went into labour, we were visiting Munem's parents. The pains were coming in waves and, as I began to feel worse and worse, I went into one of the bedrooms to lie down. A doctor friend of Munem's was visiting at the time and Munem seemed far more interested in entertaining him than in what was happening with me. My father-in-law, Hassan, was very kind, he kept coming in to check on me and he was clearly getting worried – far more worried than my own husband. There was only a small fan in the stifling room and I was overcome with the heat and the pain. A neighbour came in to see how I was and my mother-in-law jerked her head scornfully in my direction and said to her friend, 'She doesn't look so pretty now, does she?' I was in too much pain to even feel hurt by this seemingly callous remark.

Munem's guest eventually left but my husband had still not come in to see how I was. As the pain intensified, my father-in-law left my side and stormed out to Munem. I could hear him shouting at Munem, calling him names and insisting that he get me to a hospital immediately. I was helped to the car and Mazin and two of Munem's sisters crammed into the back. Every jerk of the car, every bump, every stop and start made me feel terrible and as we approached the hospital, I realised that I was agonisingly close to giving birth. The contractions were almost constant and as I bore down, gasping, Munem finally seemed to realise that the baby was about to be born. He looked at me, almost accusingly, 'You took a lot longer than this with Mazin!' He'd obviously thought there was no urgency and that I'd be in labour for a long time yet. That was clearly not the case and it was hardly the time to enter into a lengthy discussion about the relative differences in my two experiences of labour. All I could manage was a breathless, 'Of course, because he was my first-born. It's different this time!'

A woman doctor at the hospital quickly took charge of me and tried to make me comfortable. Munem left to go back to our apartment to get the clothes I'd set aside for the new baby. Our precious girl, Nada – her name means 'dewdrop' in Arabic – was born before he got back. It was April 1, 1966. Munem seemed to have been gone for hours and, when he eventually turned up with the baby clothes, I wanted to know what had taken him so long. He looked sheepish and seemed apologetic. 'I got talking to my friend, the one who's a chemist. I called into his shop.'

I was disappointed in him. Any other man would have rushed straight back, not wanting to miss a moment with his wife and new baby daughter, but I was just too exhausted to argue. 'It's not good enough, Munem,' I sighed. 'It's just not good enough.' His sister Khania came to stay with me at the hospital at night, supposedly to see to the baby while I rested, to help me look after myself and the baby, and to wash the nappies. It was common practice to do that; a mother or sister or close woman friend would help out, especially in the first few days after the birth. My sister-in-law, however, seemed far more interested in chatting to the women at the other end of the ward than helping me so I looked after my own needs and those of my baby. Within a few days, Nada and I were back home anyway and all of my friends came to see us. Mazin was delighted with his sister and she was an adorable baby.

Life seemed good again and with Mazin at school I had a lot of time to devote to Nada. Her birth may not have made Munem and I as close as I'd hoped, but things were still good. Perhaps life should have taught me by now that such happy times don't always last. Munem came home from work one day with an announcement: he was being sent back to France to work on another project. We'd have to give up the apartment and the children and I would have to move in with the family again. He seemed to feel it would be easier for me to cope with two children if I was living with the family. Our furniture would be coming with us. His mother and sisters coveted our new gas cooker – it was both a novelty and a luxury to them because they'd had to cook on primitive and ineffective paraffin burners which were low to the ground, so you always had to crouch down to use them. I thought they were dangerous contraptions and always hated having to cook on them. So, yet again I packed up our belongings and we moved to Karradah.

With Munem's departure for France, I felt as if I'd become his family's drudge. My day would begin with the school run – I'd have to stop at four different schools to drop off Munem's younger sisters and my son. But one benefit was that this marathon school run did take me close to parts of Baghdad where friends worked and I'd often stop for coffee with them and then meander back in my own time. The only problem with that was when I got back home, my mother-in-law questioned me thoroughly, about everything. Like many women of her generation, she hadn't had a proper education and couldn't tell the time so, even when I said I'd be back at a certain time, it meant nothing to her. The round of questions would always be the same: 'Where have you been? Who did you see? Where was that? What did you do?' They were never questions asked out of kind curiosity, or to show an interest in me and how I enjoyed spending my time. It was more like a mini-interrogation every time I walked through the door. Now that I could drive, it was very convenient for her to have me go out and do the school run – but not so convenient when she thought I might actually be going out enjoying myself.

I felt like I was almost expected to lead a Cinderella-like existence, doing most of the housework, helping the family, knowing my place somewhere near the bottom of the pecking order. Umm Faleh insisted on doing the cooking – obviously thinking my culinary skills were inferior to hers – but she was happy to have me there during the day to do the chores, instead of waiting for her daughters to do them when they got home from school. They'd always complain about how tired they were and how much homework they had to do. Even with Munem abroad, Faleh in the army and Bedri sadly passed away, the house was still overflowing with people: my parents-in-law, their two younger sons, all of the five daughters, Khania's children, me, Maz and Nada.

Khania's husband was in the army and stationed in Jordan. They couldn't afford a place of their own yet and, besides, he only seemed to come back often enough to get her pregnant again. They did eventually move out of the family home because Faleh bought a piece of land just one street away and Munem was contributing to the cost of building a house on it. Family always looked after their own, no matter what – or so it seemed at the time.

Khania would always stand up for her husband whenever anyone in the family criticised him for not being able to support her and leaving her almost permanently pregnant for her family to look after her and her children. She never allowed any of them to undermine him or put him down and I respected her for her loyalty. I once asked Umm Faleh why she had given her eldest daughter in marriage to a poor, ugly man, a humble soldier with so few prospects. I'd been told that Khania had been very beautiful as a young woman and could surely have had her pick of eligible men. But Khania wasn't given a say in the matter and married him without question because he was her mother's choice.

'Boys used to follow her everywhere when she was young,' said my mother-in-law, 'and I was worried she might get into trouble.'

'So you married her off to the first man who came calling?' I asked.

'Yes,' was her unrepentant answer.

So in a sense, I wasn't the only one who had suffered from

this matriarch's strong will. But knowing that was little consolation in the chaotic, stressful household. With such a big family, the laundry and the washing-up seemed endless and it always fell to me to do it. The dishes had to be washed in a big bowl outside, with cold water from the garden tap. I had to use sawdust instead of dishwashing liquid because Umm Faleh didn't want the chemicals in the commercial washing-up products to affect the orange trees when the dirty water was poured around them. If I wanted hot water, I had to boil it and carry it out to the washing bowls. I began to feel that I was going quietly mad. I felt angry and alone, furious at Munem for leaving me and the children here and missing Mum terribly. I couldn't sleep at night, I'd toss and turn, feeling tense and anxious and hating the persistent mosquitoes whose bites would bring me out in red, raw welts.

The only time I found any peace and solitude was when the rest of the house was asleep and my insomnia drove me to late-night television. I could curl up undisturbed and watch Egyptian and American films. They were my only solace. The Egyptian films were all love stories and many featured the two biggest Egyptian film stars of the time – the heart-throb Omar Sharif and his wife, a famous actress, Faten Hamama, with whom he had a young son. These were stories of blissfully happy love, impossible love, unrequited love. Evidence of happy, loving marriages, it felt to me, was in short supply around here. My parents-in-law, who were cousins, had simply married because they were told to and they'd continued to have children until Umm Faleh's menopause intervened. Her husband was a good and kind man but I'd watch my mother-in-law sometimes and wonder what life would have been like for her if she'd had other opportunities, perhaps had a good education and gone out into the world instead of being tied to an early marriage. Her father had died when she was a child and her step-father had treated her as little more than a servant, seeing her only value as someone to help look after the sons he later had with her mother.

It was little wonder that Umm Faleh had become embit-tered with age and experience. She was a tall woman with long, slim legs and she always wore the gold anklets which she received as gifts on her wedding day. They were the only possessions with which she'd begun her married life and she wore them with pride. I always thought of them as a very unlikely, very sexy accessory on this austere woman. There was no doubt that she was intelligent, she managed a large household on very little money and wanted better for her own children. But life had toughened her and, if there'd ever been a spark of joy in her, it had long been extinguished.

Many poor Iraqi women could expect little more than Umm Faleh had in her young days. Schooling wasn't a priority when their families needed them to do menial work, often as servants and only for a pittance. Then they'd be married off as soon as possible. One of my sisters-in-law, Madeha, took me to just such a wedding in the street. Next door to Munem's parents' house was a collection of sun-baked mud-brick dwellings with palm-frond roofs known as *serifa,* where poor people had set up home. Makeshift communities like this would spring up wherever there was an expanse of government-owned land. Often there'd be upwards of eight or ten people living in two rooms. We entered through the high door that led into a large, open courtyard with simple rooms leading off it. In one room, the bride-to-be, a beautiful young girl, sat dressed in her white gown. I was shocked to see her sobbing as if her heart was breaking into pieces on what should have been a happy, exciting day.

'What's wrong?' I whispered to Madeha. 'Why is she crying like this?'

'She's just found out that the man she's about to marry is not the man in the photograph that she was shown, the one whose marriage offer she believed she was accepting.' This poor girl had been tricked into thinking that her groom was a handsome young man whose photograph she'd seen. Instead he was the boy's much older, unattractive brother. I felt so sorry for her. What a way to start your married life, on a foundation of despair and dishonesty, knowing that you had no way out.

My own marriage was preoccupying my thoughts. Munem had been away in France for three months – it had seemed like an eternity for me. I was overjoyed when he got home but if I'd expected his return to magically sweep away my unhappiness I was sorely disappointed. He threw himself back into his work routine, justifying that and the fact that we were still living with the family by saying we needed the money to save for the house we were building on land we'd recently bought about five minutes' drive from the centre of Baghdad. Until we could move out, I resolved to keep busy, to take my mind off things. I went back to work for a while – just short stints here and there, filling in for a secretary friend when she went on holiday for two weeks, doing secretarial work for a lawyer, working as a receptionist for a dentist and also doing occasional interviews for the radio station.

It was only a matter of time, I told myself, until we could move out and I'd soon be back in a home of my own away from this oppressive atmosphere. I felt sure that once we had our own house life would improve; the children and I would feel more settled and Munem and I could again regain the closeness that we'd once had. I was certain of it. But the months stretched into four years. While the routine of my life was grinding on in the same pattern, Iraqi politics seemed to be in a permanent state of change. In April 1966, President Aref died in a helicopter crash and was succeeded by his brother, Abdul Rahman Aref. But two years later, in July 1968, Arab nationalist and Baathist army officers staged a coup and the President was sent into exile. A leading Baathist, Ahmed Hassan Bakr, became the new president of Iraq and within days, he'd ousted his non-Baathist allies. Saddam Hussein was the rising star of the Baath party and had already become its assistant secretary-general. It was no great surprise when he was promoted to deputy chairman of the governing clique, the Revolutionary Command Council. His main duties included overseeing internal security. The Baath party had strong ideals – one of its slogans was 'Unity, Freedom, Socialism' – and many Iraqis hoped it would herald a stable, progressive government after years of political in-fighting and turmoil.

All I wanted was an end to the turmoil I felt inside me. I'd often sit out on the porch at my in-laws' house, desperate for some peace and quiet, day-dreaming and longing for a glimmer of real happiness and stability to return to my life. I'd look at the garden, its orange trees and date palms, and wonder how long it would be before I could have a garden of my own. One day, my day-dreaming was interrupted by Assarm, who handed me a letter. Seeing the familiar red and blue markings of an airmail envelope, I tore it open to devour Mum's latest news from home but what I read rendered me speechless. It wasn't a letter from my mother, it wasn't even a letter to me. It was a candid love letter from a woman – I'll call her Anita – to my husband. There was no mistaking the intimacy of it.

My hands were shaking as I turned the pages. My heart was pounding and, although I was dimly aware of someone inside the house shouting to me to come and help set out the meal, I couldn't move. I was in total shock. So this was what he'd been doing on all of those many trips away, trips that lasted for months on end. I'd been back here, looking after our two children, putting up with being little more than a drudge for his family and he'd been living the life of a carefree single man enjoying an affair with this woman. He'd even given her his family's address so obviously he couldn't have cared less whether he got found out. It seemed so brazen and brutal. He must have known that I'd find out, or if one of his sisters had seen the letter, that they'd have taunted me about it.

When Munem got home from work, he couldn't argue with the evidence when I thrust the letter at him but he insisted that it had just been a brief fling, totally meaningless and was long since over. But why had she written to him? Why had he given her the address? How could I trust him or believe a word he told me after this? He stubbornly refused to discuss it any further and I was left to my rage and my tears. I felt I had no choice but to just block it out as best I could. He and I did not refer to Anita's letter again. Some nights, I used to sit with my father-in-law out in the garden, where he liked to relax in the cool night air. He had a favourite orange tree that he nurtured very carefully but, no matter what he did, it never bore fruit – until one year, when a single perfect orange appeared on one of the branches. He'd sit and admire that orange, following its progress day by day, looking forward to the moment when it was the right degree of ripeness and he'd pluck it from the branch and savour it. But one day he went out to check on its progress and it had gone. One of his younger sons had ripped it from the branch out of sheer spite. I knew how my father-in-law felt.

All of the children seemed to have a difficult relationship with their father. I could never understand why. Their mother dominated the household so completely that they seemed to see him as almost an irrelevance. He was a quiet man who kept his thoughts to himself and he was never a strong presence in the household. I thought of him as being a good father, a good provider. He worked long shifts as a police officer, where he'd have to stay in the police station during the week and only come home for his days off. He didn't seem to make any demands on anyone and he had few pleasures in life. One had been watching that orange grow; another was sitting in the garden of an evening, listening to his radio and sipping arak, an alcoholic drink that is hugely popular in the Middle East.

Arak is known as the 'milk of lions' because it's so strong. It's a big favourite in Lebanon, Jordan and Syria, and there are variations in the ingredients depending on which part of the region you're in. In Iraq, the drink was made from fermented date juice. I occasionally sat outside with Hassan, sipping arak and chatting. I enjoyed the gently increasing sense of numbness that the alcohol allowed me, blunting some of the sharpness of my life just for those moments. Sinuous Arabic music played on the tinny little portable radio. I ignored the disapproving looks of the women of the family, who were hovering at the door, watching us drinking and chatting. They clearly thought it was inappropriate for me to be out there drinking with my father-in-law. To hell with them all, I shrugged. The arak taste was sharp on my tongue but with each mouthful, I was past caring.

7. A Mother's Love

The dawn of the new decade, 1970, was also the start of a new era for us as a family. We moved into our own home, at last. I was so happy to have my own space, where I could live my life and bring up my children away from the interference and influence of Munem's family. I'd hoped this move would put all of that behind us. Our new home was off Palestine Road, one of the main arterial routes in Baghdad. The land had once been a sprawling graveyard but the gravestones had all been bulldozed to make way for the new housing development. I always hoped it would not be a bad omen to be living above a burial site.

New neighbourhoods were being built all over Baghdad and often took their name from a particular profession or industry – the Airline Quarter, the University Quarter, for instance – whose workers generally lived there. Our home was one of the first to be built in the new development that would become known as the Engineers' Quarter.

The Engineers' Society – a cross between a trade union and old-style British Friendly Society – had sold the building plots to its members. For just 70 dinars – a bargain we could afford with a little help from Munem's brother, Faleh – we bought a plot of 6,500 square feet. We had applied for a government loan of 4,000 dinars, enough to build the home of our dreams, but we got just half that. I couldn't hide my disappointment. Munem was such a loyal and tireless worker for his government; he gave it everything he had but, at times like this, that didn't seem to matter at all to the bureaucratic civil servants working in Iraqi officialdom. We were just another file, just another loan application.

Still, with 2,000 dinars we were able to build our home. It was simple, it wasn't ostentatious or luxurious, but it was ours. The development was so new that the roads were still unpaved. From the road, a big iron gate opened onto our long driveway leading up to the front porch and the main entrance. From the front door, you entered the sitting room. A double wooden door led from there to two bedrooms with the bathroom in between – one bedroom for Nada, who was four by now, the other for Munem and me. The dining room was directly behind the sitting room and the kitchen was next to that. This was one of my favourite rooms because I'd designed it exactly as I wanted it. The units had been especially imported from Europe and were made from a warm walnut-coloured wood. I had a favourite Syrian-made, brown embroidered tablecloth, which covered the matching table and chairs. I thought they gave the kitchen the warm and welcoming atmosphere that I wanted to achieve. The floor tiles were green with a speckled-gold surface and had been manufactured by a Czechoslovakian company that was in Iraq, building the Taji gas installation project. I liked to think they gave the kitchen a glamorous look. There was a separate store room/utility room next to the kitchen. This was where we put the washing machine and freezer and stored the richly-coloured Persian carpets in the summer when they were no longer needed to provide warmth on the tiled floors.

A staircase led from the dining room up to Mazin's bedroom where, like a typical football-mad 11-year-old, he soon covered the walls with pictures of his favourite players and teams. He worshipped Kevin Keegan, the Liverpool and England player. The stairs also led up to the flat roof, where I'd hang out the washing and where the water storage tanks were set up. In summer, I'd love coming up onto the roof to sleep in the cooler night air. It was a very common sight on the Baghdad rooftops in summer – entire families settling down for the night on mattresses dragged up to the roof and placed on bed bases left up there. It was often the only way to get some rest in the hours between the oppressive heat of the day and the early sunrise. I'd look up into the sky and muse for a moment that those stars were the same ones Mum might be able to see back in England. I'd wonder whether she too would be looking up at them now. The expanse and beauty of those starry night skies never failed to move me and, in a strange way, made me feel closer not only to my mother but to God even. It never failed to calm me and I'd fall asleep to the sound of the date-palm fronds rustling in the wind.

For the first few weeks after we moved in, the house saw a steady stream of friends and neighbours. Our social circle was widening with every year we spent in Baghdad and many of the neighbours here were people we'd first met at clubs and parties. Most of us were a similar age group, many had children, others were newly married and yet to start a family. Our immediate neighbours were Sabah and Sajda and their four daughters – how they longed for a boy with each new pregnancy. Opposite us were Seta and her Armenian husband and their son and daughter. When their daughter was a baby, I'd watch them load her into the car and drive around Baghdad until she was asleep. It was the only way they could settle her. Seta, too, had links to Karradah – her mother worked in the medical clinic next to Munem's family's house there and we often went to her for inoculations and treatment. Seta was a modern Iraqi woman, a Christian with a more western outlook, so I always felt she understood me better than some of my other neighbours.

The move to the Engineers' Quarter also brought us nearer to old friends from the Birmingham University days, including Ramsey and his new wife, Shifa, a paediatrician, who lived just behind us. On the other side of us was Basheer, who had just returned from his studies in the United States. He'd fallen in love with the architecture there and had his house built in the American modernist-inspired style. It was very nice but it didn't have the conventional flat roof that was so common in Iraqi houses so he'd be deprived of the feeling the rest of us had as we fell asleep with nothing but those stars above us throughout the long, hot summers.

Less than a month after we moved into the new house, Munem came home from work and announced that he had to go back to France on business. 'You and the children,' he said, 'will live with my family while I'm away.' My heart sank at the prospect of yet another long absence and being thrust back with his family again. I knew that I had to make a stand now, once and for all, even if it meant risking his rage by defying him. 'Never! I will never go and stay one night under their roof as long as I live.' He was determined but I was even more determined. I knew he didn't like the thought of the children and me being alone in the house in his absence and that he felt we'd be more secure with his family. But I was never going to return to those days when I'd been under their thumb, when there were endless quarrels with his sisters and mother. It was exhausting, always having to fight my corner with them, always having to be on my guard.

My upbringing hadn't prepared me for their nastiness and their tricks. I'd been an only child, much loved by my parents and spoiled by them. That upbringing had never prepared me to know what it's like to be constantly under siege, feeling unloved, rejected, manipulated and undermined. Munem knew only the barest details of what I'd had to put up with. What would have been the point of telling him more? I could have told him about their pettiness and mean-spirited comments and actions. I did tell him once about the time I found a voodoo doll with pins stuck into it under my pillow while I was staying at his parents' house. I dismissed it to him as a silly prank but I'd been astonished at their nastiness. I well remembered how it had felt to finally sink gratefully into bed one night after the tensions of another day there and then to feel something hard beneath the pillow. I lifted it up and found this nasty little totem.

Predictably, his sisters never admitted it but I knew it was them. It couldn't have been anyone else in the house. 'How can you claim to be good Muslims,' I'd challenged them, 'when you use something like this?' I couldn't help but wonder where they'd even heard of things like voodoo – some book perhaps, or one of the Egyptian films that were on television? After the girls denied it, I turned to Munem's brother, Bedri, and, even though I knew it wasn't him, I demanded, 'Well, did you put this under my pillow then, Bedri?' He looked as shocked as I'd been when I found it.

When Munem saw how determined I was not to move back in with his family, even for a few weeks, he gave way – one of the few occasions when I was able to overcome his domineering stubborn streak. But my decision actually led to an improvement, of sorts, in my relationship with his mother and sisters: they respected my independence, even if grudgingly, and I felt that I'd clawed back some of the power and self-worth that they'd sapped from me. It happens so often, when you're living with someone or close to someone, they know you're dependent on them and they take advantage of you, psychologically. But when you finally stand up for yourself, they have to respect that. You give them no choice.

Besides, I could see that, as Munem grew more successful and influential in his job in the ministry, more and more people wanted things from him, especially his family. They'd want me to act as a go-between, use my influence with him for a favour or something special. In their eyes, I had this power all of a sudden and, while I didn't abuse it, I did relish knowing they'd have to take me a lot more seriously now. Munem left for yet another trip abroad but I barely had time to miss him. I had the children, my friends, and my social life. It was such a cosmopolitan atmosphere – the Engineers' Quarter became home to people from all over the world, many of whom worked on contracts for the Iraqi government or with foreign companies. I felt that this was somewhere I could be happy and had a sense of belonging that had escaped me so far during my life in Baghdad. I was a people-watcher and here I knew everyone and I thrived on the sociable atmosphere. Looking back, these were carefree, privileged times for educated professionals in Baghdad. Could everyone have really been as happy and satisfied with their lives as they seemed? At the time, I thought so.

There were endless opportunities to socialise, with new clubs and leisure facilities springing up everywhere in the city. Each area had a swimming pool and I loved to take the children to cool off in the long, sultry summer days. Some public pools had women-only days but, at other times, there wouldn't be many other women there. Some conservative Iraqi women would have found it unacceptable to swim with men around and the more modern ones were often out working. But there were a few who were liberated enough to defy convention and others were westerners; mostly, these were the women I'd see at the pool with their children.

I loved driving all over Baghdad along the palm-lined boulevards and winding back streets, shopping, bargain-hunting, visiting friends for coffee and cake. I never for a moment felt vulnerable as a western woman driving or shopping on my own. Male drivers would occasionally try to intimidate me by speeding up and driving very close to my car but I'd laugh it off. It was their idea of a game; I'd speed off and, when they caught up with me, just do the same to them. After shopping and lunch with a friend, I'd come home to the afternoon routine: turn on the radio and listen to the BBC World Service. I loved to hear the presenters' perfect diction and Alastair Cooke's *Letter from America*, and the music and the features and especially, the news – refreshingly uncensored and international. The radio would provide my soundtrack for the daily chores: cleaning, tidying, and washing the floors and even the driveway outside, to settle the ever-present dust. The daily routine would be interrupted by the traditional afternoon break, a Middle Eastern version of the siesta. At 3 p.m. most people would end their working day and go home to eat. They'd rest and by five o'clock be up again and, fortified by tea, would be ready for the evening ahead.

I visited Munem's family only twice while he was away and I couldn't help noticing that they treated me with greater courtesy, more like a visitor – gone were the quarrels and criticism that I used to hear. They were pleasant and polite to my face, but although I knew that it was only superficial, I could deal with that. I didn't expect anything else: they couldn't change and I wasn't going to. Munem's absences became a little easier to bear, with my hard-won independence from his family and my determination not to live with them again. But also a new friendship was to sustain me more than any other during my time in Iraq. I made friends with Dalal, a wonderful woman who taught English at the school attended by Munem's younger sisters. Her husband, Adnan, worked with Munem and, like my husband, had also been sent to Britain to get his degree, though in Manchester rather than Birmingham, where Munem had studied. Our husbands often travelled abroad on the same delegations and could be away for weeks, sometimes months at a time.

Dalal and I had an instant rapport; we understood each other so well. She was tiny, barely five-foot-tall without the very high heels she used to wear all the time. She was a whirlwind of enthusiasm and fun and laughter. We saw each other every day. She'd visit me and, while I prepared the evening meal, she'd tell me about her day, recounting stories about school life, interspersed with cooking tips, and the kitchen would echo to her infectious laughter. I'd often look at her in awe, wondering where she got her boundless energy from, especially as she had a thyroid condition that she'd been warned would require life-long medication.

Dalal and I and our children would often take drives around different areas of Baghdad. She was a Shia, like the majority of Muslims in Iraq, and once drove us past one of the holiest of Shia sites, the dazzling turquoise and gold mosque rising up in stark contrast above the nondescript buildings in the narrow streets of the Kadhimiya suburb in northern Baghdad. The mosque's cluster of domes and minarets dominate the skyline in the area. It's home to the Imam Ali shrine where, according to tradition, Imam Ali, the son-in-law of the Prophet Mohammed, visited the mosque in the seventh century and dug a well there. Water is still flowing from the well and pilgrims go there, believing it has curative powers.

My husband's family were Sunnis and I learned a lot from Dalal about the differences between her branch of Islam and my husband's. When the Prophet Mohammed died in the early seventh century he not only left the religion of Islam but also an Islamic State in the Arabian Peninsula. It was the question of who should succeed the Prophet and lead the fledgling Islamic state that created the divide. The larger group of Muslims – which would become known as Sunni – elected Abu Bakr, a close companion of the Prophet, as their next caliph or leader, and he was duly appointed. However, a smaller group – the Shia – believed that the leadership of the Muslims was a divine right of the family of the Prophet and so they wanted his son-in-law, Ali, to become the caliph.

Dalal was very knowledgeable and great company; she always had something interesting to do and say. There were times when I'd bemoan the fact that our husbands had the kind of all-consuming jobs they did, that left them stressed and exhausted, and took them away from their families so much. 'Why can't our husbands be normal like everyone else's?' I'd demand of her.

'Pauline,' she'd say, serious for once, 'it's because they have this vision of making Iraq a better place to live in, a more advanced society, using all of its incredible natural resources in a way that really makes a difference.' I knew she was right, of course, even if it was easy to lose sight of such lofty goals in the everydayness of marriage and family life.

I was beginning to branch out more, stretching my mind and broadening my horizons beyond the home. I started visiting the British Council, the cultural and social hub for the British ex-pat community. I'd borrow books from the extensive library and would often settle in there, in a quiet corner, with a cup of good tea and read the newspapers in full, without the distraction of the heavy censorship imposed by the Iraqi authorities who'd ensure that articles they deemed troublesome were literally cut out from every copy before the papers were put on display in the shops. Foreigners also flocked to the British Council. It was famous for its English language classes, the best you could find, and numerous companies, as well as the Iraqi government, sent their employees there to learn English.

The British Council always felt like a classic slice of Britain set down in Baghdad. The huge garden was beautiful and strolling around the grounds the scent of roses and jasmine seemed to follow you everywhere. It reminded me so much of English cottage gardens and how often I'd ignored them back home. Now they seemed quaint and beautiful, treasured memories of home. Cocktail parties were often held on the manicured lawn and it was a wonderful place to meet all kinds of people – diplomats from embassies in Baghdad, visiting VIPs, other ex-pats and British actors or writers who might be appearing at cultural events at the British Council.

It was good to have distractions like that when Munem was travelling so much. He and Dalal's husband had been in France for three months and, by the time they returned, we were almost used to not having them around. But Mazin and Nada were excited about seeing their father again; they stationed themselves at our big iron front gate, waiting impatiently for their father's car to come into view. 'He's coming!' shouted Maz, running towards me to let me know. As Munem's driver brought his suitcases into the house, the children showered their father with hugs and kisses, but were desperate to see what presents he'd brought them from Paris. As the bags were unpacked, the children raced to their rooms to try on the clothes that he'd brought home. I too got some beautifully designed and stylish outfits, but so did Munem's sisters – he'd bought us all the same things but in different colours. I guess it was a mix of male impatience and efficiency – buy it all in one go – but it would have been nice every now and then to have something special that he'd bought with just me in mind. We took the clothing gifts over to his sisters a day or so later but I felt certain they didn't really appreciate them. Piles of clothes that Munem had bought them on his travels seemed permanently heaped up in their bedrooms, and stayed there unworn.

Munem had barely had time to unpack when the steady stream of people began to flow through our house, all needing to see him; our home was like his second office. I served them endless rounds of tea and cake and thought this was part of the price to pay for being married to someone who was doing so well as an executive in the Gas Administration.

But just as life was settling back into its usual pattern with Munem home with us again, out of the blue he said that he thought it was time I took the children to England to see my mother. Nada was five now, he reasoned, and she'd never even met her English grandmother. It had been seven years since we'd last been back. I was surprised that Munem had suggested it but very happy to be going back. I wrote to Mum, telling her the good news and again trusted to fate that the letter wouldn't be delayed in the painfully slow Iraqi postal system or simply disappear. You could never be sure that letters sent abroad weren't read and re-read by the Iraqi authorities.

Maz and Nada were excited about the prospect of their big trip, Nada's first in an aircraft. Mazin was old enough to remember his last visit to England but he'd be looking at it with different eyes now he was so much older and also sharing it with his sister for the first time. Despite the age gap, they were very close. Mazin was the perfect older brother, always patient, always protective of Nada. He had a real talent for making things and, when he was younger, would spend hours quietly with his Meccano set, building elaborate constructions. Even as he got older, he never lost that love of diligent craftsmanship. Obedient, gentle Mazin just adored his father; Munem was his hero. Where Mazin was quiet and gentle and introspective, Nada was more often like a mini-whirlwind of energy and noisy activity. She couldn't bear to sit quietly and just amuse herself, she was too busy racing around. Nada worshipped her brother and was happy to follow his lead – except if she had other plans of her own, like escaping from her grandparents' house if someone forgot to close the gate properly. She'd run around the corner to Khania's house in the next street where, much to Nada's delight, she could always find a cousin or two to play with. Munem always said that Nada was more like me in looks and temperament, while he thought that Mazin took after him.

When we set off for England, the excitement that both Maz and Nada felt was contagious and got us through the flight from Baghdad and the long train journey from London to Halifax. They didn't complain once and just seemed to take in everything with wonder: the scenery viewed from the train, the endless green fields and the styles of buildings that were so different from the Iraqi landscape and architecture. Mum was thrilled to see us and especially to meet her granddaughter for the first time. She put a lot of effort into making us welcome but it was clear she'd lost a lot of weight and I wondered if her rheumatoid arthritis had got worse. We talked for hours, long after Mazin and Nada had gone to sleep, catching up on everything from family news to the latest twists and turns of our favourite TV programme, *Coronation Street*.

The next day, we went shopping and the children's perfect manners soon disappeared when confronted by shops full of things they'd never seen before, different games and toys and gadgets that you'd never be able to buy in Iraq. To get some peace, we sent them to see a film while we finished our shopping, leisurely strolling around the markets and shops just as we'd done when I was a child. When I was a youngster, I'd spend alternate Saturdays with my parents – one week, shopping with Mum, the other week, off to the football with Dad. That day I'd been walking around the same shops and markets with my own children in tow. It was a happy and relaxing start to a month's holiday during which we saw the local beauty spots and visited our relatives. Towards the end of our month, it was clear that Mazin and Nada had had enough. After the initial novelty had worn off, they grew bored and felt stifled in the insularity of quiet, conservative small-town England. They didn't have any friends, didn't know anyone their own age and they'd been used to a different life in Iraq where they'd had so many friends and so much freedom and wide open spaces in which to roam. At home, Maz could go pheasant-shooting or horse-riding with his uncle, Assarm; they'd all go to the open-air cinema or swimming in the Tigris or the many public and private pools. They missed their father and their school friends and made it very clear they were ready to go home.

But just as our holiday was drawing to a close and the day neared when we'd be flying back to Baghdad, I got a letter from Munem that changed everything. He had written to say that he didn't want me to come back to Iraq, that the children and I should stay in England and make a life for ourselves there. He said our marriage was over. This seemed an extraordinary turn of events. Through my tears, I wrote back immediately and demanded explanations, insisted that he tell me what was going on and begged him to think about the children. How would they react to suddenly being told that their father had insisted that they couldn't go home to him? What about their schooling? How would I support them on my own here? Where would we live? The three of us wouldn't be able to stay indefinitely with my mother in her one-bedroom flat.

For all the questions I heaped upon Munem in this letter, I was also asking myself what could possibly have brought this on. There'd been no hint of it when we left and, if it had been what he wanted then, why wasn't he man enough to come out and say so? Had he resumed his affair with Anita or embarked on another liaison? Was it the family's opposition to me? Was the Baath party uneasy about him being married to a British woman? Had I become a political and professional liability? The questions tumbled round and round in my head until I could think no more. It was maddening to have this one-way conversation in my mind and not have him here to talk to directly. We'd both made mistakes, I knew that, but this was not going to be the way to resolve them. We'd been together since we were teenagers, we'd been through a lot to get to this point, we'd had two children together and now he was throwing it all away in a letter.

Our return plane tickets expired and I had to make excuses to the children about why we weren't going back as planned. I wrote to Munem's brother, Faleh, trying to find out what was going on. I knew Munem loved his children. I had no doubt about that at least, even if I barely entered into the equation where he was concerned. A month went by and just when I began to doubt that I could keep up the subterfuge and I'd have to tell the children the truth, I got a letter from Faleh, telling me to come back and enclosing new tickets. There was no explanation and no word from Munem but at least this way we'd be going back to Baghdad and I could find out what had been going through his mind. I wanted my Mum to come back with me now even more than ever. I needed her and I didn't want to leave her. But she couldn't be persuaded, so yet again we said our sad goodbyes on her doorstep. Perhaps after all, I didn't have the courage to stay behind in England, but I did have the courage to go back to Iraq. I was ready to face whatever was waiting for me.

8. The Rise of the Baath Party

Baghdad airport was busy when we arrived but, through the crowd, we could see Munem waiting for us. Maz and Nada were so happy to see him. I wondered for a moment if their obvious delight in being with him again had made him feel in the least bit sorry for having written that letter suggesting the three of us stayed in Britain. I just didn't know how to greet him or what to say beyond 'hello'. Like so many things in our lives, the letter he'd written was never discussed. When he didn't want to address a problem, he shrugged it off as if it didn't exist. In retrospect, I realised that that attitude was to sum up our life together.

When we got to the house, I saw it was very neat and tidy; his sisters had been in to give it a good clean before our arrival, as if to say an uncharacteristically warm 'welcome home'. And it was good to be home. I had missed my space, my own things, my friends and my neighbours, who all came to see me to find out how the holiday had been. They said we had a new neighbour, an Egyptian woman, Su'ad, a widow, who had been married to an Iraqi. You must meet her, they urged. The first chance I got, I did go over and introduce myself to Su'ad who had four children, aged from four to fourteen. We liked each other immediately and discovered we had close mutual friends. Su'ad had not had an easy time of it. She told me that her husband had been killed while working in Kuwait; he'd been crushed by the tractor he was driving. She had always promised him that, if anything happened to him, she would take the children back to Iraq, to the house he'd built for them all, and that she'd bring up the children here. She was now fulfilling that promise.

As the sole breadwinner, she worked as an English-Arabic translator and was also very involved with the Baath party, by now the hub of Iraqi political life. The party had a wide network of social activities and had begun to dominate many spheres of everyday life. Her work for the party was all-consuming and she wasn't able to spend as much time with the children as she would have liked, but that was part of the price she had to pay. The Baath looked after its own and she knew that. I thought she managed things well, considering the responsibilities that she had. But, when I visited her one day, I realised that I was not the only one who had problems with Iraqi relatives. When I got there, she ushered me into the visitors' room – the Arab equivalent of a reception room set aside for entertaining guests – which I thought was rather formal, given our friendship. We'd normally just chat over coffee in the kitchen. But I understood the reason when I walked into the room and Su'ad introduced me to her husband's brother, who was visiting from Hilla, a village in northern Iraq.

'Hello, pleased to meet you,' I said to him while Su'ad went to the kitchen to get tea and cakes. He was a man in his mid-50s, about five feet two, balding and with a paunch. I couldn't help noticing that he had rather bad breath. Su'ad came back with the tray and asked him politely, 'How is the family?' I could tell by the tone of her voice and her demeanour that she felt uncomfortable with him but I couldn't tell why. I looked at her, trying to work out what was going on.

'Fine, thanks,' he replied with a brief smile. After a bit of small talk and some awkward silences, Su'ad went out to the kitchen to make more tea. When she returned, she leant over to place her brother-in-law's full teacup on the small table next to him and, as she did so, he reached out and touched her hand. Su'ad jerked her hand away with such ferocity you'd have thought she'd just been bitten by a snake. It was clear that she was upset about something but it was impossible to find out what it was while her brother-in-law was sitting here. I had to be getting home anyway and politely made my excuses and left. Within a few days Su'ad was at my door in tears. I made tea as she blurted out the reason she was so upset. 'My husband's brother came back and took the children to Hilla and I am alone in the house,' she said, holding her tea as if taking comfort from its warmth but not taking a sip. He'd asked her to marry him and, when she refused and would not relent about her decision, he was furious. He'd taken the children as punishment, saying they should be with her husband's family. I didn't know how to console her so I sat holding her hand until her tears dispersed a little and she calmed down.

'I keep hearing tapping noises on the windows. Whoever it is runs away when I put the outside lights on. I keep them on every night now,' she added. I could see the tension and anxiety etched on her face.

'Look,' I said, 'give me a ring when you hear them next time, and we'll catch them together.' But she never did call and her children never came back to live with her. Her husband's family kept them in Hilla. Su'ad had to give up her fight for them and return to Egypt. As soon as she'd gone, her brother-in-law came to her house and took all the furniture away. It made me feel so sad for her. Once in the grip of these Iraqi families, I thought to myself, always in their grip, especially if you're a woman, an outsider, and they didn't choose you as their precious son's wife. You had to be a very strong woman to try to break out of that stranglehold and those who did often paid the price and ended up losing their children to the husband's family.

Never one to stint on wielding her own considerable influence in such matters, my mother-in-law, Umm Faleh, clearly thought she'd have better luck with a daughter-in-law that she'd chosen rather than with me. Munem and I were summoned to the family home to discuss her favoured candidate as a bride for Faleh. She was desperate to see him married off and settled with a family. The woman in question, Bushra, was a distant relative but I'd never heard anyone mention her before, least of all Faleh, so the fact that she was to be his bride was something of a surprise to all of us, including Faleh. His mother was so busy with her plans for his marriage that she didn't even think to ask him for his opinion. Faleh's firm response when she finally did was, 'But I don't want to get married!' I could see he was clearly upset that his future had been hijacked in this way.

It was not the first time it had happened. When he was a handsome young student in the Soviet Union, he'd fallen in love with a girl there but she was deemed unacceptable by the family and when he finished his studies it was out of the question that their relationship could continue. Back in Iraq, he eventually met someone else and wanted to marry her – a real love match, not a marriage of convenience as many were – but his family ruled that she too was unsuitable and he'd been too weak to go against their will. These days, the reasons for his reluctance to marry were more practical. He'd confided in Munem that he'd discovered during a routine visit to the doctor that he had a heart condition. It could get a lot worse as he got older, he reasoned, and why burden a wife and children with the worry of that? Faleh was insistent that no one else in the family must know about his health worries. Perhaps he just didn't have the energy to keep challenging his mother and her plans for him, so he agreed to the marriage.

We all went to see Bushra and meet her family and were ushered into the visitors' room, where we were offered refreshing, cold drinks while the hard bargaining got underway in the customary discussion of financial terms for the marriage and for any possible divorce. It seemed both unromantic and eminently practical, especially in a social system where love was considered an optional bonus in marriage – if you were very lucky – and not an essential as it is in western culture. People of the same generation as my parents-in-law would have seen love as an unnecessary distraction, clouding one's judgment.

Faleh's initial reluctance and doubts melted away when he started spending time with Bushra; she was charming, intelligent and fun to be with. She came from a progressive family, her father was a retired army officer. Bushra always dressed in the western style even when she was out in public, unlike many Iraqi women who still favoured the black silk *abaya*. I had to admit that this time my mother-in-law had been right about something – Faleh and Bushra's 'arranged' marriage did become a love match and it was clear to us all that they were very happy together.

The new school term came around and Mazin, who was now thirteen, went to a high school near our house. When he was younger, I'd always planned to enrol him at Baghdad College, the elite private secondary school which had been opened by a group of American Jesuit priests in 1932. This was where many of Iraq's wealthiest and most prominent families sent their sons. After initial suspicions that the Jesuits had come to convert Muslim youngsters, people soon realised that providing an excellent education was the order's priority and that Muslim, Roman Catholic, eastern Orthodox, Jewish and Protestant pupils were welcomed equally. The school had superb facilities. The Jesuits' approach to education was so popular and successful that in 1956 they opened a second college, Al-Hikma University.

Against the odds, the Jesuits had weathered many political storms in Iraq since the 1930s and even when the United States embassy closed during the 1967 Arab-Israeli War and American citizens were urged to leave Iraq, the priests had ignored the warnings and stayed. It was only when the Baathists came to power in 1968, that the Jesuits' fate was sealed. All private schools were nationalised and the priests at Al-Hikma were ordered to leave Iraq in November that year. Hundreds of their students defied the authorities and went out to Baghdad airport to say goodbye to them. Less than a year later, the priests at Baghdad College also faced expulsion. They were given three days to leave the country or face the consequences. They had no choice but to go. The State took over the running of the school.

Saddam Hussein later enrolled his two sons, Uday and the younger one, Qusay, at Baghdad College. I'd eventually hear such bad things about the two of them that I was relieved that Mazin wasn't at the same school, let alone associating with them. I'd been told that Uday – the more dangerous, unstable and obnoxious of the two – routinely carried a gun in class and he made no secret of the fact that he'd use it with impunity. Qusay was quieter, not as obviously aggressive and brutish in the way that his brother was. But both knew that no one dared to challenge them for fear of the retribution of their father, who thought his beloved sons could do no wrong. They could ignore every rule and the teachers were able to do nothing but pander to them. The brothers had a fortune to spend on flashy clothes and cars. Their bodyguards crammed into the classrooms on the orders of the boys' security-conscious father and their presence disrupted the lessons for the other students. But many parents felt they couldn't take their children out of the school because questions could be asked about why an exclusive school that was good enough for Saddam Hussein's sons was not good enough for theirs.

Neither boy was especially bright and they treated schoolwork as a joke but they usually managed to gain astonishingly high marks. On one occasion, it was said that Uday demanded more time to finish a test in class; the teacher duly extended the time for everyone by 15 minutes but when he finished within just a few minutes he insisted that the teacher stop everyone else as well. In the coming years, the full scale of his depravity and the sons' abuse of power would be revealed. Uday, especially, considered women to be little more than disposable playthings even when he was just a teenager. Years later, we found out that a school friend of Nada's had been raped by them while they forced her fiancé to look on, powerless to intervene – apparently a favourite tactic to humiliate both the man and the woman.

Maz's new school wouldn't have the same facilities as Baghdad College, I knew, but I wasn't sure what the standard of education would be like now it was under Baathist control. The tentacles of the party were spreading everywhere, in youth groups and women's groups, and I didn't want him to become embroiled in political activity. I could see what turmoil and instability politics had caused in Iraq. I put Nada in a new school too, now that her big brother would be leaving the one they'd both attended. Throughout her school days so far, he'd always been her protector and now she wouldn't have that. Nada was very interested in ballet so I put her into the new Baath party-run School of Music and Ballet. A lot of the tutors were from the Soviet Union and, with their rich classical dance heritage, I felt sure she'd do well.

There were big changes for Munem too. His hard work and dedication had been rewarded with a promotion from the Gas Administration to the Ministry of Oil at a time when plans were being made to dramatically overhaul the Iraqi oil industry. It had long been controlled by the Iraqi Petroleum Company, a consortium of the world's biggest oil companies – British Petroleum, Shell, Esso, Mobil and Compagnie Française des Petroles. This dominant role of foreign companies in managing the extraordinary potential of Iraq's oil industry had outraged many Iraqis and successive governments had tried to challenge the IPC's stranglehold but with only mixed success. The issue of possible nationalisation had been rumbling for some years and the government had taken steps to find alternative partners, including the Soviet Union. Saddam Hussein himself, now a senior figure among the Baathists, was taking personal charge of overseeing the path to nationalisation and Munem's ministry would play a key role in his strategy. Iraq had the world's second-biggest oil reserves, and the government wanted – in fact, desperately needed – to use the almost limitless wealth that could be generated by such reserves, to fund a sweeping nationwide modernisation programme.

The Oil Minister at that time, Murtada al-Hadithi, was eventually sidelined and replaced by Tayeh Abdul Karim. By virtue of his job the minister was also chairman of the Iraqi National Oil Company but he knew next to nothing about the industry. He'd previously taught English and only got his lofty job because he was a high-ranking Baath official; such was the power of the party that it could transform

LEFT: This photograph of Munem was taken in 1956 in Halifax, where he was doing his 'A' Levels, before going to university.

BELOW: Munem in Birmingham with Abdul Hussein Hakim, Barbara's husband.

ABOVE: Mazin and I in Mr and Mrs Ora's back garden, in Birmingham. Mazin was born on 20 November, 1959.

LEFT: Munem in Baghdad, enjoying a day off from military training, in 1961. I was still in England, and he sent me this photograph of himself.

ABOVE: Dancing in the open air at the Engineer's Union, in Baghdad.

BELOW: Mazin on the roof of our refinery house.

ABOVE: Mazin on the bonnet of our old Fiat, with Bedri in the driving seat, in Karradah.

RIGHT: Mazin and I on the porch of the house in Dora.

BELOW: Mazin standing outside our house, in Dora.

ABOVE: Bedri and Mazin in Karradah.

RIGHT: Munem, Mazin and I cooking musgoof, a flat-river fish, in Karrahada. I was four-months pregnant with Nada.

BELOW: Falah at the back with his black Mercedes. In front, from left: Assarm, me, um-Falah (my mother in law) with Nada in front of her. Khania's three daughters: Tharmara with Isra in front of her, then Eman. Munem's sisters Emel, Hashmia, Madiha, Faliha and then Mazin in front.

Munem, third from left standing next to Saddam Hussein.

Munem making a speech at a seminar in Baghdad.

LEFT: Mazin and
Nada on the porch
of our house in the
Engineers' Quarter
on Palestine Road,
with Kizzy on
Mazin's lap, 1982.

RIGHT: Mazin on a
break, in Habannia.

LEFT: Nada in
Melbourne, Florida,
in Atlantic Street,
in 1993.

a humble English teacher into one of the most influential
government ministers in the entire cabinet. The minister
was a pleasant and decent man, who lived just around the
corner from us. I always noticed that he carried his comb in
the top pocket of his jacket; it seemed such an unlikely
thing for a government minister. I often wondered how
someone so mild-mannered had managed to rise up the
ranks of this omnipotent party. For all intents and purposes
it was a one-party state – you didn't get anywhere in Iraqi
life if you weren't a member and it affected all aspects of
day-to-day life. Munem had of course joined the party but
he wasn't a dedicated Baathist so would probably never
have the same meteoric career path as his ineffectual boss,
even though his knowledge and experience was so vastly
superior to the minister's. Munem was appointed under-
secretary to the minister but in fact, he did the minister's
job in all but name.

If Munem had ever tried to elbow his way into the
governing clique – that inner sanctum of the Revolutionary
Command Council (RCC), full of yes-men and slavish disci-
ples – he would certainly have had a good chance of the top
job but he could never bring himself to do that. He worked
so hard, it would have been natural if he'd sought the job of
minister but then it would have meant being at the very
heart of Saddam's growing power base and Munem would
soon begin to have nagging doubts about Saddam's abilities
to lead the Iraqi people. A post on the RCC was only offered

to a select few of Saddam's top henchmen and he would later cement their total loyalty in any way that he could – including expecting them to implicate and involve themselves in the same brutality, violence and repression for which he would become infamous. Munem would never have been capable of such things and he recoiled at so much of what he heard emanating from the senior leadership. I'm sure that he eventually felt that the ideals he'd clung to – making Iraq a better country, giving Iraqis an improved standard of living, giving them control of their country's oil riches so that all Iraqis could benefit – were being betrayed and the opportunities squandered.

I did wonder sometimes whether another reason Munem never became minister was even simpler – he was married to me, an Englishwoman, a foreigner, a Christian and not a Baath party activist like so many Iraqi women at the time, who would have been seen, in senior government circles at least, as being far more appropriate consorts than I. Perhaps Munem himself resented me in a way and that's why he took his frustrations out on me with his infidelities and his bullying tactics. I saw even less of him than usual as he wound up his work at the Gas Administration and began moving into new offices at the Oil Ministry. But I filled my days happily enough and there was always plenty to do while Maz and Nada were at school.

I was about to set off to do some errands one day when I realised the car keys weren't in the place where we always kept them. I looked everywhere; they'd disappeared. The car itself was locked but the back window was down slightly and I thought if I could just manoeuvre it a bit further, I could unlock the door and see if the spare key was in the glove-box. The window refused to budge but then I remembered the old coat-hanger trick that you see in films. Inside the house I found a wire coat-hanger and when I'd untwisted it, I could ease it through the small gap at the top of the window and use the curved end to hook around the door-lock and pop it up.

I leaned across and opened up the glove-box, to see if the spare key had been tucked inside. There was no key. Instead, I pulled out a large bundle of letters that had been stuffed at the back unnecessary. They had all been sent to Munem at his office address. I didn't recognise the handwriting on any of them. I opened each one and read every word. The letters were from several different women in England, France and Germany – women he'd obviously met during those long trips abroad on government business. In some of the letters, these women professed their undying love for him and in others they described in very graphic detail having sex with him – what they'd done and what they planned to do when they saw him next. I felt nauseous. I actually felt that I was going to be sick; the physical reaction was so strong. He hadn't even bothered to throw away these letters, he'd kept them perhaps as some kind of trophy that flattered his male vanity and his ego, or had these women actually meant something to him? I could well believe the former, but struggled to believe that he'd felt anything more than lust for them. Perhaps, I told myself clutching at straws, they'd just been a way to pass a few lonely nights while he was abroad for months at a time. But the letters had such a familiar tone and were so intimate and explicit. They can't all have been one-night stands. He may have kept the letters, perhaps wanting me to find them so he didn't have to confess. But then again, perhaps he'd hidden the car keys so there was no danger of me getting in to the car and discovering them.

Everything seemed to cave in around me. I began to doubt so much, and to wonder about things going back to our days in Birmingham when he was at university, little incidents here and there which I'd just dismissed as my imagination playing tricks: furtive glances exchanged at parties, a bit of flirtatious behaviour at times. There was the woman who lived close to where Munem had been staying when he was working in northern Iraq: when I spent a week with him once, I'd noticed a woman standing outside her house as if she was waiting for someone. Moments later, the phone rang and Munem answered it, mumbling something and then telling me he had to go out. I had such a strong feeling that he was going out to meet this woman; I couldn't explain it but I just felt it. There'd also been a secretary at the United States embassy in Baghdad who'd paid a little too much atten-tion to him for my liking, but I hadn't taken her seriously –

at the time. Now it seemed everything was suspicious. Had I really believed Munem when he'd tried to persuade me that Anita had only been a holiday fling that day when I'd read the letter she'd sent to his family's house? Another letter from her was among the ones I'd just found so he'd obviously been lying to me about ending that affair. Were any of these women the reason why he hadn't wanted the children and me to come back from England that time? Despite all evidence to the contrary, I had to keep telling myself that he still loved me – in his way – but what I was no longer certain of was whether that was enough for either of us. If he had a need for these other women, I thought, what does that say about me?

When he came home from work that night, I flung the letters at him and demanded an explanation. For a moment he looked sheepish, surprised he'd been caught out yet again, but then he went on the defensive, insisting it was all my fault that he'd needed other women in his life. He seemed unrepentant and arguing about it got us nowhere. My head was full of 'if only' – if only he'd told me about all of this when the children and I were in England. I could have decided to stay there permanently if I'd known the extent of his betrayal. I wouldn't have been hankering after the life we had in Baghdad. Now I wanted to go back to my mother. If he wanted me out of his life, I'd leave once and for all. But Munem refused to let me go. The next two weeks were spent in a daze of tears and confusion. Just when I thought there could be no more nasty surprises, a parcel was delivered to the house. It had been sent to Munem at the Gas Administration but because he was still in the process of moving to the Oil Ministry and between the two offices at the time, the package had been sent to him here at home. I didn't even hesitate before opening it. Inside was a pair of Munem's shoes and a loving letter from Anita in Germany. He'd left the shoes at her house when he'd been staying with her during a recent business trip. One phrase in the letter kept going through my mind over and over, 'Make love not babies!' I threw the opened parcel, the shoes and the letter on our bed so Munem would see them as soon as he walked into the room.

Cornered again with evidence of his infidelities, Munem once more made a half-hearted attempt to dismiss it as a passing fling and simply said, 'She and I are finished. I don't see her any more.' This woman had surfaced yet again and while it felt as if she had suddenly started to dominate my life, I resented the fact that she was living her life in Germany, completely unconcerned about the chaos she was helping to cause. So I wrote to her, telling her to get out of our lives and out of my marriage. To my surprise, she actually wrote back, saying that she hadn't even known that I existed. She said Munem had lied to us both: he'd told her that he was divorced. I was frustrated and angry, feeling that I was trapped in a no-win situation. I couldn't stay with him and I couldn't leave him. A part of me simply shut down, deep inside, and became separated from the rest of me. I became this person who, on the outside, was smiling and sociable and coping, but deep inside I felt very different. I learned to keep a part of myself back, away from the world. It was an act of self-preservation and it saved me.

9. *The Gathering Storm*

Munem had refused to let me go back to England when I'd so desperately wanted to leave but, when his sister Hashmia became ill, he insisted that I take her there to see a specialist. Hashmia had been to countless doctors in Baghdad, some of whom couldn't find anything specifically wrong with her, while others prescribed steroids for the swelling around her joints and the pains in her neck and one told her that her ailments were largely psychosomatic. He said the medication she was taking for a non-existent illness was in itself making her feel awful. Hashmia refused to accept the diagnosis and Munem defended her, 'My sister wouldn't invent an illness. The doctors don't know what they're talking about,' he told me. I felt the doctors *did* know what they were talking about but, if it meant seeing my mother again, I'd indulge my sister-in-law and take her to England.

Hashmia was admitted to a private hospital in Harrogate for a barrage of tests and I went up to stay with Mum, but made the bus trip to Harrogate several times a week. It was tiring and devoured the time that I wanted to spend with my mother. Our time together had become ever more precious after I found out that she had cancer and the outlook wasn't encouraging – at worst, she could be with us for only another year, maybe two. I was stunned when her doctor told me. It explained why she'd lost even more weight and seemed so tired all the time. I knew she wasn't immortal but I wasn't ready to lose her yet, I couldn't lose her yet. We had too much of life left to share with each other.

Hashmia left hospital when the tests were completed and the doctors assured her they couldn't find any serious problems. I longed to stay with Mum and spend more time with her but I couldn't let Hashmia go back to Iraq on her own. I felt responsible for her; she'd never travelled before and I knew she wouldn't be able to cope. In the few days left before our departure, we visited my relatives, and I took her to see the quintessential English seaside resorts of Blackpool and Brighton. I showed her the ballroom in Blackpool, where I'd gone many times as a teenager. In Brighton, we strolled along the West Pier, enjoying the afternoon sunshine and we danced at an outdoor tea dance. We went into the bar at the end of the pier where a pianist played the hits of the day and old classics. Hashmia and I sat in the sun, luxuriating in the warmth on our skins, and we talked, having what I would call a real conversation for perhaps the first time, for once seeing each other as individuals, away from the tensions and rivalries that had enmeshed me in Munem's family home.

Away from her home environment, I could see more clearly that Hashmia was a deeply unhappy woman and her real or imagined health problems had little to do with it. She'd had a loveless marriage to a relative, a lot older than she was. The marriage had of course been arranged by her mother, but it had failed miserably. Hashmia and her husband argued constantly. They hadn't had children, which was another source of tension between them, and finally her husband left. He soon remarried. The whole experience had left Hashmia very bitter and coloured her view of life, love and marriage forever. But with me in England, she had her first taste of real freedom away from the dictates of her family. One important thing did change for her while she was in England. She took off her traditional black *abaya* and never wore it again.

I left my mother with the promise that I'd come back as quickly as I could. Half a day later, I was at Baghdad airport, where the whole family had turned up to meet me and Hashmia. To my surprise, Munem was there and appeared happy to see me – an increasingly rare occurrence when his life seemed dominated by work even more than ever. His ministry was at the forefront of one of the most sweeping reforms ever to hit the Iraqi economy. The government had, as promised, taken the dramatic step of nationalising the oil industry in June that year, 1972. A new law set out the programme of nationalisation that included the State's acquisition of all properties, rights and facilities relating to oil operations. The Government knew it was something of a gamble and they had taken some steps to try to off-set the resulting loss in revenue from the Iraq Petroleum Company (IPC): they hadn't nationalised subsidiaries of the consortium and they had also introduced a package of austerity measures, although ordinary Iraqis didn't seem to mind feeling the economic pinch – in fact, they celebrated the achievement of wresting back an industry that was so vital to their country's future. With their own oil revenues under their control, Iraqis were therefore in a much stronger position to control their national destiny and develop their country into a modern, twentieth-century nation.

Saddam had been carefully laying the groundwork in the months prior to nationalisation with a visit to the Soviet Union for talks with the Prime Minister, Alexei Kosygin, in February of that year. He'd gone as the personal envoy of President Bakr. Armed with a number of proposals, he returned with a deal all but done. Two months later, Iraq and the USSR signed a treaty of friendship and co-operation, guaranteeing that the Soviets would buy Iraqi oil. Saddam had calculated that this too would soften the blow of any retaliatory action launched by the IPC consortium when nationalisation was due to be announced in June. He was right. Saddam further consolidated the Iraqi government's hold on the country's oil with a trip to France, soon after nationalisation was announced. There, he met President Georges Pompidou and persuaded the French leader to accept nationalisation in return for concessions for French companies who wanted to invest in the Iraqi oil industry. Saddam emerged triumphant as the one person who'd done more than any other to secure Iraq's oil fortunes for itself and to break the stranglehold of the foreign oil companies, with rallying cries like 'Arab oil for the Arabs!'. At home he was fêted as a hero and abroad became known for the first time as a major player in Iraqi politics. Many Iraqis believed that Saddam Hussein already had his sights set firmly on the presidency and that now he was just playing a waiting game.

The power and status of the Oil Ministry was enhanced by the demise of the Iraqi Petroleum Company and Iraq's new-found powers to negotiate its own international contracts for development and investment in the oil industry. And Munem was now at the very heart of it all. But for all the exciting developments at work, there were some serious family problems too. His mother, Umm Faleh, had a heart attack and needed a lot of help during her recovery. All but three of her children had left home by now and the older ones were too busy to look after her, so it was decided that I should do it. Neither she nor I were exactly overjoyed at the prospect but Munem installed her in our bedroom and, with the doctor's instructions ringing in my ears – she needed plenty of rest and a nutritious low-fat, salt-free diet – I set about nursing her back to health. She didn't like my cooking and I could hardly blame her; I'd never claimed to be one of the world's great chefs but basic, bland low-fat, salt-free food was something I could manage. Umm Faleh pulled a sour face with every spoonful, probably half-suspecting that I was trying to poison her to even up a few old scores.

Besides she had another target now – her daughter-in-law, Bushra, who could do no right in her eyes. I was surprised to hear Umm Faleh being so critical; Bushra had been her choice of bride for her son, after all. But I think she'd realised that simply choosing her son's bride was no guarantee that she'd have a good relationship with her. Still, it was something of a relief for me to see that the woman I'd always thought of as the mother-in-law from hell was equally unforgiving of all her daughters-in-law, whether or not she'd arranged the marriage. None of us would ever be quite good enough, it seemed. This could so easily have been an opportunity for me to enjoy some pay-back time but, despite her cussedness, Umm Faleh's vulnerability and helplessness made me see her in a more compassionate light. And she too seemed to acknowledge that I was a person in my own right, with worries and fears like anyone else. When she was feeling a bit better, we'd go up on to the roof and sit in the cool, night air, looking up at the clear skies above us and talking. She asked about Mum and was genuinely sympathetic when I said how worried I was about her and about how the cancer could progress.

Hashmia had obviously told her mother about my life in England and about meeting Mum and my relatives when I'd taken her back for medical treatment.

At other times, my mother-in-law and I would sit on the roof and laugh at the antics of the squirrels as they climbed the luxuriant date trees Munem had planted in the garden, a gift from a dear family friend. Without even realising it, after all these years, she and I had come to an under-standing: two old adversaries who actually didn't dislike each other nearly as much as they thought they did. It had been a slow progression to reach a place of respect and affection but we managed it. In many ways, I had a better relationship with her, woman to woman, than she had with her own daughters. They didn't have much time for her once they had families of their own but I made an effort and my children were always a source of great happiness for her. Mazin and Nada visited her often and always sat with her and talked to her; they showed a real interest in her as a person and were very respectful and considerate. They shared a loving bond with her that I just didn't see between her and the other grandchildren. Maz and Nada never ignored her or were cheeky, or simply ran riot when they visited, the way the others usually did.

Umm Faleh was inundated with visitors during her recovery – friends and relatives from near and far, some of whom I'd never even heard of, let alone seen before. Her half-brother was among them, only he wisely decided to leave his Egyptian girlfriend, a dancer, in the car when he came in. Umm Faleh would not have approved of her brother going out with a dancer – and nor I suspect would his wife and children if they'd known. My mother-in-law enjoyed all the attention and was recovering well, even though she seemed to take great pleasure in defying the doctor's orders about her medication. While I was cleaning one day, I discovered a cache of tablets under the bed. She should have been taking them each day but she'd simply been dropping them on the floor when no one was looking. I felt that, if she was well enough to show such devious reasoning and to think she didn't need her medication any more, she was well enough to go home. She agreed.

The family's relief at my mother-in-law's full recovery was overshadowed, however, by worries over Faleh's health. He was taken to the army hospital in Abu Ghraib, just to the west of Baghdad, for routine tests to try to find what was causing his bouts of breathlessness. We all went to see him when he was first admitted and he looked fine and was in good spirits. But we became increasingly worried at the way he seemed to deteriorate so rapidly once he was in hospital. I suggested taking him to England to see one of the many eminent heart specialists there but, given that he was still in the Army, we were told that he would have to remain in the military hospital as a matter of protocol. That was all very well, I thought, but the family should at least have a say about where and how he was treated. After all, they had his best interests at heart whereas to the military doctors he was just another patient.

When I went to see Faleh one evening, he looked jaundiced and every movement seemed to be an effort. He was clearly getting worse by the day and there was just no explanation for it. The male nurse came in to give him his medication but it didn't seem to make any difference. The nurse returned just as I was leaving, bringing a resuscitator unit with him. I was reluctant to leave Faleh but I had to be getting home. As I walked down the corridor, I noticed that many of the darkened wards were empty. It seemed quite eerie. Sadly, Faleh died the next day. Minibuses ferried people from all over Iraq to Baghdad for the three days of mourning. The men all went to the mosque to pray for Faleh; among them were high-ranking army officers, longtime friends of his.

The women and children crammed into his house to pay their respects to his wife, Bushra. She was distraught and I didn't know how she'd cope, left alone as a young widow with two sons under the age of two. The boys would grow up with barely a memory of their father. Bushra could count on little support from his family. Faleh had been so well-loved; he'd been a kind and decent man, tough on the outside and soft and loving on the inside. He'd loved my children as if they were his own and was always so patient and attentive towards them. Munem too commented on this once and in a rare moment of emotional insight, he said that he didn't know how to love people in the open and unconditional way that Faleh was able to. His comment was very revealing. If you have that degree of insight, I thought, why don't you ever act on it to improve the way you relate to us? Munem was never an overly affectionate father. He always bought the children wonderful gifts when he was away on his travels; there was never a time when he didn't bring them back something special. I think it was his way of expressing his love. He found it easier to do it through material things than in showing his emotions.

We never did find out for certain whether there was anything suspicious in the sudden deterioration in Faleh's health. In our worst moments, we speculated that he could have fallen foul of someone very senior in the army and been poisoned, or simply not been given the best of care at the army hospital. It was too late anyway. His body was taken to Samarra for burial in the family plot. After Faleh's death, his mother didn't visit Bushra or make an effort to see her grandsons. If they want to see me, she'd sniff, they can come to visit me. The death of her favourite son hurt her so deeply that she no longer wanted to be known as Umm Faleh, mother of Faleh. It was too painful a reminder of him to hear his name whenever someone addressed her in that way.

From that time, she preferred to be known as Hajia – an honorary title that Muslims are able to take after they've been on the Hajj, the pilgrimage to the Saudi Arabian city of Mecca, the birthplace of the Prophet Mohammed and the holiest city in Islam. Munem's parents had been on the Hajj when they'd gone to Saudi Arabia with his sister, Faleha, who worked there for a year. The pilgrimage is something every Muslim is required to do once in their lifetime and because of this, it's a hugely important event for them. My mother-in-law found it an immensely uplifting spiritual experience, but she told me she was disappointed with the way so many of the pilgrims she saw that year seemed to be more interested in going shopping for televisions and other electrical goods, than in doing their devout duty.

Still grieving for Faleh, we were so focused on family issues that political developments barely touched our lives. The head of the internal security services, Nadhim Kazzar – one of Saddam Hussein's closest associates – had launched an abortive coup attempt at the end of June. Kazzar had developed a fearsome reputation as the arch-torturer who instituted the brutal regime in the state security services' building where many of the g overnment's opponents were interrogated. He was one of the few Shias in the upper echelons of the Baath party hierarchy but his audacity in trying to overthrow Bakr and Saddam showed the depth of the divisions within the pro- and anti-Saddam factions within the party. He'd planned to have both men assassinated but the plan ended in chaos and soon after Kazzar and more than 30 others were executed. The crushing of the plot led to a purge of the security services and dissident elements among the Baathists. Saddam Hussein's position – tantalisingly close to taking full control of Iraq – now seemed unassailable.

The Baath party wanted to reassure Iraqis that not only was it business as usual after the coup plot was crushed, but people were safer than they'd ever been. In Baghdad alone, the authorities claimed that the emergency police could be on the spot, anywhere in the capital, within minutes of being called. Whether or not this was the case, the police were not able to stop the killing spree of a notorious murderer who'd become known as Abu al-Tubar – the Axe Man. It was thought that he didn't work alone but as part of a family gang, who carried out a series of house robberies, during which the occupants – entire families – had been hacked to death. There were even stories about the women being raped before being killed. He targeted wealthy neighbourhoods and always managed to evade the security guards and high fences that many homes had. It was more like a plot from an American horror film than scenes from everyday life in Iraq, where indiscriminate violent crime was – at that time – uncommon and a serial killer was simply unheard of. It all seemed so unbelievable. Surely Iraq had not changed so much that society could tolerate such things? What were the authorities doing to keep us all safe? People were in a state of near-hysteria, no one knew who would be next or whether they would be safe in their own homes any more.

The more I thought about it, the more I realised that there had been a slow but certain change in how we were all living. It had once been very common to see people out strolling in the evening; neighbours would call in on one another and sit in the garden or on the roof terrace, sipping tea or something stronger. It had always been a part of everyday life here but increasingly you didn't see people do that much any more. There was a general, almost indefinable sense that Iraq wasn't quite as safe as we'd always thought. A lot of the British women I'd known when I first came to Iraq had gone back home. Some of the other foreign wives had also left.

If Munem was away, our next-door neighbour would kindly invite us to come over and stay there so we wouldn't be on our own in the house. His family, like several others, had decided it was safer to sleep on the roof terrace. We did go to their house once and settled down to sleep on the roof but were kept awake all night, not by fear but by the nervous jabbering of the women of the house, who were startled by the slightest noise. Other people abandoned their usual habit of sleeping on the roof, believing that Abu al-Tubar could be using the door from the roof into the house to gain entry undetected. I thought we'd be safer at home: our windows had bars on them and our doors were sturdy. I kept the doors locked when the children and I were in the house, and the keys were always in my pocket, never left lying around. The tension in the air was almost palpable. We all wondered how much longer it could go on.

The days felt a little safer, simply because there was more activity and many more people around, always coming and going. One morning, after Munem had gone to work and Maz and Nada were at school, I went out into the garden. With the door locked behind me and the key safely in my dressing-gown pocket, I dead-headed the roses, enjoying their rich old-fashioned perfume, and inspected the grapevines and the fruit trees. I heard a noise and turned to see our neighbour's official driver open our gate and walk up to the outdoor drinking-water tap in our garden. He cupped the cool water in his hands and drank. He didn't say a word to me, although I saw him every morning when he came to pick up our neighbour, Basheer. He'd always smile and say hello but today was different. I was surprised at his insolence but my instincts told me not to challenge him. He turned from the tap and walked to the door, reaching up to the handle and tried to open it. It was locked, of course. I could feel the key in my pocket. The man turned and saw me watching him. He stood there, giving me a sinister smile. My heart was pounding and I was rooted to the spot; I could not move a muscle. We stared at each other for what felt like an eternity but was probably only a few seconds. The silence was broken by a ringing bell out in the street, the regular call of the man who came delivering the bottles of gas that we all used for cooking: 'Abu Nuffat, Abu Nuffat!' I could hear him shouting out his signature call – 'the paraffin man, the paraffin man!' My neighbour's driver turned and walked quickly back down the path. If my heart hadn't still been pounding with fear and the adrenalin surge, I might have even convinced myself that I'd imagined this encounter.

A few days after that the doorbell rang and, after first checking who it was, I opened it to see two shabby beggar-women asking if I had any bread to spare for them. They looked pitiful and I noticed that one had her arm in a sling, just as my mum had had after hurting her arm before she went into hospital. The sight of this really tugged my heart strings so I gave them a little something to help them on their way. It was common for beggars to come to the door, asking for food or old clothes. No one thought anything of it; you gave them what you could and I didn't imagine there was anything sinister in it – until much later.

There were a number of incidents that made us all feel on edge. Neighbours had unsolved break-ins. The burglaries always happened at odd times, but when homes were empty, even if only for a short time. It was as if whoever was committing the crime knew the movements of people in the area. One night, when Munem and I had begun to make love, I saw someone peering in through the window at us. I pushed Munem away and ran out to see who it was. Far from being some teenager playing a prank, it was a man in his early fifties who paused as he made his get-away, just long enough for me to see his face. It was disturbing but I managed to push it to the back of my mind until I was watching the television news one evening and saw faces I vaguely recognised in a report on a series of burglaries carried out by a family gang of criminals. Among them were my neighbour's driver and the two women who'd been disguised as beggars, and the Peeping Tom who'd been spying on Munem and me.

The local burglaries had indeed been done by people who knew the area and the patterns of daily life in the neighbourhood. They'd all been monitoring our movements and knew when to strike. It seemed that they were also linked to the Abu al-Tubar gang. I felt that I had had a lucky escape. It emerged that Abu al-Tubar was a former henchman in the internal security service. It was said that he and his gang initially evaded capture because they were able to keep one step ahead of the police, thanks to his intimate knowledge of the top-secret radio frequencies and codes used in police communications. Many ordinary Iraqis had believed the horrible crimes were the work of the security services and that the authorities had used the widespread fear sparked by the attacks as a way of keeping people insecure and worried about the future. If people were frightened and wanted to be protected, they'd readily accept any measures that the government might deem necessary to maintain law and order.

The panic around the Abu al-Tubar killings seemed to go on for a long time. The long drawn-out fear and anxiety over this crime wave had really unsettled people in Baghdad. What was to stop it all happening again? We needed something to help us regain our confidence in law and order and a civilised society and our faith in our political leaders. World events began to work in the government's favour. Oil prices were soaring as the Arab oil embargo began to bite after the outbreak of the Arab-Israeli War in October 1973, when Arab members of the Organisation of Petroleum Exporting Countries (OPEC) along with Egypt and Syria announced that they would not ship petroleum to any countries who expressed support for Israel in the conflict – primarily, the United States and its allies in the West. While western countries struggled to control the dire effects of the embargo and ever-increasing oil prices, money from this new-found oil wealth poured into the Iraqi government's coffers, thanks largely to the nationalisation of the industry a year earlier. Saddam Hussein had been the architect of that strategy and he now set about using the oil money to fund tangible benefits that all Iraqis would be able to see around them – a modernised infrastructure and sweeping health and education reforms. Iraq embarked upon a period of extraordinary social and economic transition. Munem always said that the oil would not last forever and Iraq couldn't rely on this to the exclusion of everything else; it had to develop in every other way as well.

Electricity projects brought power supplies to many villages for the first time. There was a building boom in cities and towns all over Iraq, and new hospitals, health clinics and schools sprang up. Iraq already had a strong professional class – doctors, dentists, lawyers, engineers and teachers – but the government recognised the need for further development across the whole of society and an educated and skilled workforce from the bottom up. It did everything possible to encourage students to go to new colleges to study agriculture, the arts and sciences, and to learn trades. There was a huge effort to reach across all social classes and groups, especially those who'd never before had the means to pay for college or vocational courses, or hadn't had access to a proper education. There'd been compulsory education laws for many years in Iraq but those laws had never really been enforced until now.

The government also launched ambitious literacy programmes. Classes were held at local schools in the evenings and there were programmes on television to help people improve their reading and writing skills. The ones who benefited most from this were women who hadn't had the chance of a formal education. Lessons were compulsory so the more traditional and conservative husbands and fathers, especially in the poorer urban areas and the countryside, couldn't stop the women in their family from learning to read and write. In a significant way, it eroded some of the control that these men had exerted over the lives of the women. For the first time ever, many of these women had a social life outside the family circle. I too followed the classes on the television as a way of improving my Arabic.

The United Nations educational and cultural agency, UNESCO, later honoured Saddam with an award for his achievements in promoting Iraq's social development.

Women were also encouraged to join the Popular Army – the people's militia – where their duties included digging trenches for road works, and they were taught how to use a gun and drive a truck. They were also able to join the military if they wanted to. Women from poorer communities had greater opportunities for social interaction than ever before. They could learn new skills and develop their confidence. Women were encouraged not just to do new things but to think in different ways, less conservative and tradition-bound ways included abandoning their long-established habit of wearing the traditional *abaya* in favour of more modern western-style clothes. Where once poor women could have expected little more from life than an early arranged marriage to an older relative they probably didn't even love, the wider world was now opening up to them in ways they couldn't have imagined before this government initiative. While some conservative men may not have approved of education and an improvement in the status of women, the efforts to include all Iraqis in building their country's future were much more inclusive rather than divisive. Everyone in the community was encouraged to feel they had a role to play. A good future was no longer just the preserve of the wealthy, the political elite or the brightest of students. I was proud that Munem was playing his part in creating the kind of wealthy, progressive country that we wanted our children to grow up in, but there were growing signs that there might be a high price to pay for that.

10. United in Sorrow

It had been thirteen years since I'd been in England in the winter-time. After living in Iraq for so long, I'd forgotten how the chill and the damp gets into your bones, seeps into your lungs and seems to stay there. I'd forgotten how dull and draining the milky blue-grey winter light could seem. And I'd forgotten the December-long obsession with Christmas gifts, cards, wrapping paper and 'season's greetings' that seemed to pervade every surface of every shopping area in the land. The crass commercialism and the enforced jollity were so at odds with how I was feeling about being there and the reason why I'd come back. Aunty Polly had sent me a telegram to say that Mum was seriously ill in hospital and that I should come back without delay if I wanted to see her in her final days. Every other journey back here in the past thirteen years had been full of excitement and anticipation at seeing Mum at the end of my travels. This visit was marked by dread and anxiety and sorrow.

Mum was in the same local hospital where I'd been a student nurse in Halifax. I even recognised a few faces from all those years ago. Any other time, I'd have stopped to chat and catch up on everything but now my only aim was to get to my mother's bedside. She lay against the pillows, frail and tiny, every breath an effort. I hugged her and kissed her hand, willing her to keep taking those breaths, however laboured. She looked up at me and smiled, and said between gasps, 'Your skin is nice and smooth, love.' I murmured a thank you but, really, I was lost for words. How do you even begin to express how you are feeling at times like this, to convey the depth of the love you feel? It was impossible. I set about making her comfortable. The hospital was so well-heated, it was stifling and surely not making it any easier for Mum to breathe. I knew she always kept her bedroom window slightly ajar at home, even on the coldest December day, so I opened the window near her, just a fraction to let some cooling, fresh air in for her to breathe.

I stayed with her all that day and through the night, not talking much because she had so little strength left. 'We'll spend Christmas at home, Mum,' I said, trying to sound bright and hopeful, but we both knew that wasn't going to happen. I sat beside her bed and watched her sleep. As she lay there, I felt consumed by so many emotions – fear, anger, sadness but mainly guilt at not seeing her as much as I would have liked over the years. I'd often felt torn between my life in Iraq with my husband and children and my love and concern for her back here. I had had to make a choice and had tried to make the best of it for everybody. Relatives came to visit her – Mum's younger brother, Albert, and his wife, Muriel; Mum's sister, Polly, along with Polly's daughter, Sheila, and sons, Fred and Bob. They stayed for quite a while and I was grateful for their support. Mum slept and woke intermittently. The full force of the jet-lag had hit me and I knew that I too had to sleep. I whispered to her that I'd see her first thing in the morning.

'Okay, love,' she said, 'but will you straighten up those Christmas cards for me?' She gave a slight nod towards the cards that had been sent to her at the hospital and had been placed haphazardly on the windowsill, where she could see them. 'And could you just comb my hair before you go?' This was so like Mum, so neat and tidy, with such a pride in her appearance and wanting everything to be just right. They were tiny things but she was so meticulous and having a sense of order meant a lot to her. As I gave her a hug I tried not to cry or look too anxious. I could feel how frail she was. We kissed goodbye and I left her, hoping she'd have a peaceful night's rest, and looking forward to having another day with her tomorrow.

Being back in her flat, knowing she wouldn't be there smiling at me when I opened the door, was so hard. It felt cold and empty and joyless, nothing more than a shell of what it had been until so recently – a home with her at the heart of it. I looked around at Mum's possessions, her favourite things, the everyday things. All seemed meaning-less without her moving among them. I went to bed but, as exhausted as I was, I couldn't sleep. The wind howled outside and I lay there listening to it and to the loud, incessant tick of the big clock on the sideboard. I couldn't even turn on the television to distract me; the programmes ended at midnight and that was hours ago. I made some tea and sat there waiting for daybreak, feeling utterly disconsolate. When there was a loud knocking on the door, I knew it could only be my cousin, Sheila. 'It's time, Pauline,' she said, when I opened the door. 'We must go now.' Mum appeared to be unconscious by the time we got to the hospital but she opened her eyes briefly as I sat there, holding her hand. She smiled lovingly at me in one final moment of recognition and then she slipped away from me, away from everything, and was gone.

I ran to the hospital entrance where my cousin Fred was waiting; he hugged me, trying to calm me. I could hear inconsolable sobbing somewhere close by, shattering the silence of the early morning and then I realised that the sobs were coming from me, somewhere deep inside that had never been in pain like this before. Sheila insisted that I go back to her house, not wanting me to be alone right now at Mum's. Aunty Polly gave me some sleeping pills and my body gave in gratefully to them, sleeping for much of a day and a night. But when I finally awoke, it was to the reality of the arrangements that had to be made – choosing the coffin, planning the funeral. I wanted the same music that we'd played at my father's funeral in 1959. I'd been four months' pregnant with Mazin when my Dad died but, as sad as it had been to lose my father, at the time I'd had the comfort of Mum and Munem, and my new baby on the way. I knew from my father's funeral that the hardest thing was to follow the coffin to its final resting place. And now the same thing was happening with Mum. I sat there, dazed, listening to the words that were being said over her coffin and then watching it disappear, as the curtains closed around it with such frightening finality.

The next few days were spent clearing Mum's flat, with Sheila there to help me. I found things from my childhood that Mum had kept, souvenirs of seaside holidays, little items won at bingo evenings. It wasn't practical to take things back to Baghdad with me so I packed them carefully away in boxes to be stored in Sheila's loft and I dispersed Mum's furniture around the family. I'd said goodbye to Mum and now I was saying goodbye to a lot of my past as well. I closed the door for the last time on her rented flat and returned the keys to the local council who owned the building. I had no idea when I'd come back to England. My main reason for wanting to come back as often as possible had now gone and there was little left for me here. I had to go back to my future: Iraq.

There was no one waiting to meet me at Baghdad airport but I found Munem's cousin, who worked there, and he helped me to get my bags to the taxi rank outside the terminal building. I walked past the famous Lebanese singer and actress, Sabah, who seemed to be waiting for her driver. I recognised her immediately by her trademark long, bleached-blonde hair. She was one of the great divas of Arab music and film, known as *Al-Shahroura*, the Singing Bird. Her career had started in the 1940s and she was still as prolific as ever. She sat there exuding a regal presence, as if she wanted everyone to come over and acknowledge her and pay court. I knew she often came to Iraq to sing for high-ranking people in the government.

Our house was in darkness when the taxi pulled up outside. There was only the sound of the occasional stray dog barking in the street to welcome me home. The driver carried my suitcases to the porch and I dragged them into the silent house. I was too exhausted to unpack and fell on the bed, weary beyond belief. When I awoke in the early hours, Munem was undressing for bed. It was after 3 a.m. and he'd just got home. He obviously hadn't been expecting to see me. 'Why didn't you let me know you were coming? I didn't get a phone call,' he said. I had sent a message and phoned repeatedly but there'd been no answer. But in bed that was all forgotten and with his arms around me and our bodies entwined, I felt that at last I was home, safe and protected. The worries of the world, all its pain and sadness and loss, could be kept at bay just for now, just for those few hours. I sensed that Munem felt the same.

I opened my eyes the next morning to glorious sunshine, so vastly different from those dismal, grey December mornings

I'd just left behind in England. I took my cup of tea out onto the porch and looked at the lush beauty of our garden, with the roses in full bloom and the heavy scent of the gardenias enveloping me when I closed my eyes. The peace of this garden, the cycles of nature in birth, growth, decay and re-birth, comforted me. These things that seemed so transitory were what actually remained and continued, while we were the ones whose lives were so fleeting. I thought of Mum and wondered whether there really was an afterlife where we'd all be reunited with those we'd loved and lost. My thoughts were interrupted by Munem, who sat down beside me. 'I'm so sorry about your mum,' he said gently. The two of them had always got on very well. I knew he meant it and I was touched. I looked at his face, at those beautiful dark eyes, now surrounded by worry-lines and his once-black hair turning white. For all the difficulties of our marriage, the pain of his infidelities and his slavish devotion to his job, there were still fleeting moments like this that made me remember why we'd fallen in love and why, despite all the problems, we stayed together. At times like this, when it was just the two of us, I realised that the ties between us were still strong despite the strains that sometimes frayed them at the edges.

It was Friday, the Muslim holy day and day of rest, so we went to see Munem's family and to pick up Maz and Nada, who'd been staying there overnight. Munem had told the family about Mum and everyone showed a kindness and compassion towards me that I'd seldom glimpsed before. They were still feeling the pain of Faleh's death so they could understand my grieving as well. My mother-in-law gave me a big hug and told me how sorry she was about Mum. We'd both felt such loss that it made us more aware of each other's humanity, more able to understand the other's feelings. I did think, though, that it was a pity that it took so much sorrow to bring us closer together.

11. The Shadow of Saddam

The telephone rang. I could hear the nervousness in my husband's voice, in his few stilted, deferential words, 'Naam Estadi... la Estadi' – 'Yes, Sir ... no, Sir.' I knew immediately that it was Saddam Hussein on the other end of the line – there was never the need for any other words when addressing him. He called our house so frequently that my husband came to dread the sound of the ringing telephone. Munem never had a break from work. Saddam would phone at all hours of the night to demand of him, 'Why didn't you do this? What's happening about that?' Later we would realise just to what extent Saddam was able to use people but, in using them, he destroyed them. He cleverly hid his cruel streak initially; so many people – millions, in fact – were completely taken in by him.

The often intolerable pressure on Munem at work had an inevitable effect on our home life. It put our relationship under a lot of strain. Munem couldn't take his frustration out on his colleagues, or his boss, the Oil Minister, or

Saddam, of course, and so he took it out on us. He was drinking more and more, to try to relax and forget about work. Our social life was such that everywhere you went someone put a drink in your hand – at nightclubs, at parties, at friends' houses. Drinking heavily became both a habit and a refuge. Munem would drink more to try to relax but it often had the opposite effect; he'd become increasingly wound up and there'd be violent rages. At times like that, it felt as if our marriage had become a love-hate relationship, with us staying together only for the children's sake, not our own. Those times increasingly overshadowed the good ones.

When Munem arrived home from work in the evenings, I'd watch his face and carefully try to read his moods. If he was smiling, I'd be relieved because it meant he'd had a good day and, as a result, we'd have a good evening at home with no rows and no shouting. He'd show a big interest in Nada and Mazin, chatting with them and asking how their day had been and what they'd been doing at school. But if he was scowling and obviously in a foul mood, it meant that he'd had a bad day at work. My heart would sink and I knew we'd all be paying for it that evening. He'd shout at the children, 'Go to your rooms! Get your homework done!' or, if they were watching television, he'd say, 'Turn that thing off; all you ever do is watch TV!' On days like that it was impossible to have a reasonable conversation with him. One evening, not long after I got back from England after Mum had died, Munem came home from work to find me in tears in the bedroom, looking through some old photographs I'd brought back with me. They were of my father and grandfather. I was wrapped up in my memories and my sadness, and Munem was tired and angry. He'd obviously had a stressful day at work and resented the fact that he wasn't getting my attention. He grabbed the photos from my hands and before I realised what he was doing, he tore them to shreds. I was heartbroken; they were the only photos I had of Dad and they were irreplaceable. The photos I'd treasured lay in tatters on the floor.

There were other times when he was so withdrawn that he'd barely say a word. The Baath party encroached on our lives in so many ways, not just through the government. Munem often held meetings at home after work and several senior party members would turn up. My role was really only to ferry trays of tea into them. Despite the bad times, I did miss him when he was away so much on government business but he was always happy to get away from the ministry, because Saddam put so much pressure on him. I too was relieved that my husband could at least have a brief respite from the mental torture that Saddam inflicted.

There was another long trip, three months in Russia, and the children and I continued family life as usual, so accustomed were we to his absences by now. Soon after his return from Moscow, Munem came home from work and he announced that Saddam himself had invited us to join him at a lavish reception at a new club in Baghdad, the

Monsour. The reception was being held to celebrate the achievements of the all-powerful Baath party. Declining such an invitation would have been unthinkable for, while Saddam was not yet president – only second-in-command – there was no doubt about his ambitions and the unquestioning loyalty and obedience he demanded. He knew it was only a matter of time before he'd be president and all of Iraq knew it as well.

I searched my wardrobe for something suitable for such an important occasion and decided on a mauve, long-sleeved, high-necked gown I'd bought on my last trip to England. When I tried it on, I couldn't fail to notice how much I'd changed during the years in Iraq – the vibrant, shapely young woman who'd come to this country so full of vigour and energy and enthusiasm seemed to have disappeared forever. Staring back at me in the mirror was a thin, pale reflection, almost mocking the lust for life in which my younger self had luxuriated.

Armed with an embossed invitation to meet the man himself, we walked into the glittering reception. The hall was crowded with impeccably dressed women and men and we were immediately struck by the clamour in an atmosphere that bristled with anticipation, excitement and tension. Music was playing but no one was dancing; they were all waiting expectantly. Then an extraordinary thing happened: as if by some secret signal, all conversation stopped and all heads turned as our host walked in, surrounded by his ever-present bodyguards. By now, every person in the room was standing and deafening applause filled the hall.

Saddam Hussein took it all as his due and why shouldn't he? He was the most awe-inspiring man in Iraq: handsome, charismatic and immensely powerful. He had a rock-star persona that actually made some women scream and faint at his feet if he was at mass outdoor gatherings. Now, in these plush surroundings in front of a hand-picked audience, the night was his alone. We'd been told that President Ahmed Hassan Bakr would not be attending due to illness. That didn't matter in the least. As Saddam made his slow procession to the front of the room, he stopped at intervals and greeted friends and associates, the very essence of charm. Eventually, he stopped at our table. He shook hands with my husband and then turned to me. In just seconds, I took in every detail: he was wearing a fashionable French designer suit, immaculately tailored to enhance his well-toned body. His neat black hair and moustache were trimmed expertly. The perfume of impeccably subtle French after-shave wafted around me as Saddam Hussein stood in front of me and smiled, reaching out to take my hand. His soft hands and long fingers held mine firmly. I looked up into his piercing, dark brown eyes for the second time in my life. He smiled warmly at me, showing the whitest of teeth and dimpled cheeks, which gave his face a boyishly mischievous look. His stare was so penetrating, so focused that I dropped my gaze just for a moment before recovering myself and murmuring politely in greeting, 'Ahlan wa Sahlan?' – 'How do you do?'

Like every other woman in the room, I was completely drawn in by the aura of power exuded by this handsome man. I'd seen on television how women in a crowd addressed by Saddam would scream and wave at him, the way young girls used to do at the early Beatles' or Rolling Stones concerts. Standing so close to him now, I could understand why and how he could generate that kind of hysteria. When he smiled at you, he focused on you entirely, no one else in the room seemed to matter. In an environment like this he was charm personified. He smiled at me again and moved on to sit at his table, close to ours. As I watched him walk away, I could sense the extraordinary confidence of this Jekyll and Hyde character, by now in his late thirties. He commanded the room effortlessly and basked in the knowledge that he held everyone spellbound. He'd staked out his territory, surveyed his terrain and was now saying to us all, to the whole of Iraq, 'I am *the* man, I am *the* real leader, I am Saddam Hussein'.

This was the man I'd soon see in portraits, posing masterfully on an Arab stallion, depicted as a great warrior and a hero who would lay down his life to defend the people of Iraq. He wanted to be a leader who would appeal to all sections of Iraqi society, so portraits and posters would depict him variously as a devout Muslim, praying towards

Mecca, or as a man of the peasantry, in Bedouin robes, or to appeal to the Kurdish population, in traditional Kurdish costume. This was the man I'd see portraying himself as the indulgent family man, the loving husband and father, the patriarch with one or other of his three young daughters perched on his knee and at his side, his wife, Sajida, and their two sons, Uday and Qusay, smiling happily for the cameras. Children in Iraq would be encouraged to think of him as *Amo* Saddam, Uncle Saddam. He'd be photographed taking his children swimming at the popular holiday retreat he'd created, Habania. Once, he was there swimming with his bodyguards when my sisters-in-law and I went for a picnic. The men beckoned us over to say hello. We'd learn later about his legendary appetite for women and how none would be foolhardy enough to turn him down. At the time, we didn't feel at all in danger, we were just flattered.

Tonight, Saddam Hussein was the undisputed star of the show. He gave a rousing speech about how the Baath party was creating a brilliant future for Iraq and everyone applauded wildly. It would have been unthinkable to do anything else. There was no doubting that he was the architect of so much of the modernisation programme that transformed the lives of millions of ordinary Iraqis. And he made sure that everyone knew it, even before he was made president. The cult of his personality was already well-established. I couldn't turn on the television or read a newspaper without seeing Saddam on visits to various grandiose projects, or with Sajida and their five children. The Baath party gave away home appliances to poor families and Saddam could be seen on television, visiting people's homes and chatting to them about their daily routines and concerns. He did indeed come across as everyone's favourite uncle. He'd open up the fridge and admire the contents, saying things like, 'It's thanks to the Baath party that you have this food here!' After he became president, he declared that his birthday – 28 April – should be celebrated as a national holiday, and so it was, with parades and street parties and schoolchildren all over Iraq donating money to buy birthday cakes for him. In fact, many actually doubted whether Saddam even knew his birth date. At the time when he was born, the system of registering births was haphazard and illiterate peasant farmers might not get around to registering their newborn children for many months, if at all. So the Iraqi authorities assigned the babies a common birth date – 1 July – to at least provide a degree of bureaucracy, if not accuracy.

It wasn't compulsory to join the Baath party but it may as well have been; you simply didn't get on in your career if you didn't. There were different levels of party membership starting from 'endorser' through to 'follower' and beyond. Each level required a certain amount of commitment and input until you got to the senior echelons of the party when your commitment was expected to be total. Many party members were benefiting greatly from the wide-ranging system of patronage and favours. I could see first-hand how membership of the party was changing lives from a school friend of Mazin's, who lived very near to us with his mother. The boy, Hafeth, and his mother had moved to our neighbourhood from a poor, densely-populated suburb known as 'Saddam City', which had been built to house tens of thousands of people who'd been living in the *serifa* mud dwellings that had sprung up around the city. I asked Mazin how Hafeth's mother could afford a house in our area, coming from such humble beginnings and without a husband to support her. 'They're active in the Baath party and Saddam helped them get a house,' answered Maz in a matter-of-fact way, as if it was the most natural thing in the world to see such a transformation in a family's fortunes.

Hafeth came to our house a lot. He seemed to enjoy being around a proper family and looking at all of the beautiful things we had in the house. He always wanted to hang around in the kitchen chatting to me when I was cooking or listening to the radio. I felt he had a kind of fixation on me; he was very artistic and sketched me during one visit to our house. I found him an unsettling presence in the house and I was always worried that he'd be a bad influence on Mazin. Hafeth was the ideal recruit for the Baath party – a fatherless, disadvantaged, vulnerable lad, who wanted to make something of himself. The party could use his slavish devotion for its own ends and was a way for him to channel his ambitions in life just as Saddam Hussein had done. Saddam himself came from a poor background with an absent father. He was raised by his mother and her second husband, who was cruel to the boy and kept him away from school so he could steal chickens, eggs and sheep from neighbouring peasant farmers, which the family then sold.

When he was still a child, Saddam had gone to live with his uncle, who became a much-needed father-figure. His uncle was an officer in the Iraqi army, a fervent supporter of Arab nationalism, an anti-colonialist who'd spent five years in prison in the early 1940s for his outspoken pro-Nazi views. Inspired by this man, Saddam's interest in politics grew through his teenage years and he joined the Baathists. The party had given him his start in adult life and a launch-pad for his goals and dreams. So, for someone like Hafeth, Saddam Hussein's life story resonated very strongly and he was seen as the perfect role model – but he was not the role model I wanted my son to emulate.

The Baath party made it increasingly difficult for parents to guide their children and even told them not to listen to us. I was as aware as most other parents of the stories that were circulating about the party using its network of youth groups to recruit children to spy on their parents. They were told to report back on anything that could be considered damaging or unpatriotic. A chance remark could be passed on in the schoolyard or overheard by a teacher who was a Baath activist and that would be it. The next thing would be a knock on your door or an encounter with the security services in the street or at your place of work. Nada told me years later that she'd been approached to spy on her father and me but she said she'd refused. Saddam himself said in 1977, 'Teach the student to object to his parents if he hears them discussing state secrets... teach them to criticise their mothers and fathers respectfully if they hear them talking about organisational and party secrets. You must place in every corner a son of the revolution, with a trustworthy eye and a firm mind that receives its instructions from the responsible centre of the revolution...'

Eventually, you could never be sure that your home wasn't bugged, anyway. It was always best to assume that it was because such spying became routine for the Baath party. The party could get all the information it wanted, one way or another. Many of us had numerous experiences that suggested that we may have been under surveillance of some kind. Your home could never be your sanctuary when you felt that every word was being monitored and recorded, and could one day be used against you or your family.

When my best friend Dalal came to visit, I was all set to share my concerns with her, when I noticed how upset she looked. 'What on earth is the matter?' I asked.

'My husband has just been made Iraqi ambassador to Russia,' she said. 'We're leaving next week and I don't want to go.' I felt so sorry for her. It was such a high-profile post and an honour for her husband. But Dalal was happy with her life in Iraq, despite the pressures and anxieties. It was her home and now she was being forced to uproot everything for who knew how long. We sat and drank tea together, digesting this news, and listening to the music on the BBC World Service. We always hoped to hear our favourite song on the music programmes – 'Que Sera Sera' – and whenever it came on the radio when we were going for drives in Dalal's rickety old Russian-made car, we'd sing loudly together, 'whatever will be, will be, the future's not ours to see...' Those simple words were so profound in a way and they seemed to sum up so much of my life, and Dalal's. Perhaps that's why we loved the song so much. Dalal left Baghdad reluctantly but knowing she had no real choice. We promised each other that we'd spend lots of time catching up as soon as she could get back for a holiday. I knew I'd miss her terribly; she was my ally, my confidante, almost the only person I felt I could really trust.

Seemingly out of the blue, the government announced a change in the nationality laws: all residents had to take Iraqi citizenship. This affected many of the foreign wives; some countries didn't accept dual nationality and they had to make the decision about staying in Iraq or going back to their homelands. Many did return home, including friends of mine, and I heard of a number of marriages breaking up because of it. Munem's driver, Towfiq, took me down to the British embassy to surrender my passport. He walked into the building with me and we found the official who was dealing with it sitting at a desk surrounded by piles of passports on the floor around him.

'Throw your passport on the floor with the others and tell him you don't want to be British any more,' commanded Towfiq.

I spun around to face him, astonished at his presumption. 'I will never say that! I will always be British.' I did have to leave my passport there but, as I strode away, I knew that, despite the government's bureaucratic game-playing, there was far more to my identity than some official document. I could think of very few good things that an Iraqi passport could bring me, having seen the way the country was treating its own citizens.

I recalled my friend Delia, who'd come to me in tears, begging me to ask Munem to help her find out what had happened to her husband, Assard. 'He went out yesterday to buy bread,' she told me, 'and I haven't seen him since.' She knew instinctively that something terrible had happened and was distraught about it. Delia felt that someone in Munem's senior position might be able to find out information or intervene to have her husband released, if he had, as she suspected, been taken by the security forces. Munem tried to find out more details but even he was met with silence. Delia didn't give up easily; she visited us every now and then in the hope that Munem might be able to tell her something. She never saw or heard from her husband again. His only crime, she believed, was to be writing an academic history of Iraq. Even mere words, it seemed, were very dangerous things in Iraq these days.

12. Living with Fear

Munem was determined our son would excel and was happy when Mazin was accepted at Baghdad University to study mechanical engineering. It was something Maz had always wanted to do and had worked very hard to achieve. He was following in his father's footsteps with his choice of engineering, but Munem never failed to remind our son that he was expected to be the perfect son, the perfect student, to make his father proud. Munem never wasted an opportunity to remind Mazin of how hard his own life had been – the poverty of his family, how his father had had to support such a big family on a humble policeman's wage, how Munem had won a university scholarship by studying day and night, squinting under a bare low-wattage light-bulb because his mother insisted that there was no money to waste on using electricity unnecessarily. Munem pushed our son hard; it often came to blows between them and when that happened, I hated him for his harshness. He could be very inconsistent and extreme in his emotions, either very loving and kind, or enraged and violent.

Mazin was now a young man but I still worried about him and wanted to protect him. He made lots of new friends at university and brought them home to meet us. The only friend I didn't like was Hafeth. I'd watched him grow up from a boy to a man and I knew how involved he was in the Baath party. I always urged Mazin to be cautious around him and not see him very often, worrying that Hafeth would lead Mazin into some kind of mischief.

My life was beginning to feel quite empty. Mazin was at university, Munem was so involved with his work and the family had persuaded him to take Nada out of the Music and Ballet School and put her in a school next to them, where his sister, Madeha, now worked as the assistant head mistress. They said Nada would do better there, she could focus on passing her exams and have fewer distractions than at home with me.

I also missed my friend Dalal, who'd written to me, telling me she'd settled in to her busy new life in Moscow. So many other old friends had also left Iraq over the years. I could now see how women who'd never really lived their lives for themselves but only for their families could feel that life was empty once their children had left home. It was how I felt then – isolated and alone and fed up. I couldn't see myself anymore – where was *I*? I wished we could leave Iraq but we were trapped by our circumstances, by Munem's work and his position. It was like being at the mouth of a tunnel, looking in and seeing only darkness and more darkness beyond.

One of the few things I looked forward to these days was visiting the British Council to catch up on the newspapers and use the lending library. A neighbour of mine, Lesley, taught there and she'd told me about a new course – English as a foreign language – being offered, for which they needed tutors. She thought I'd be well-suited to teaching. Students, businesspeople and government employees flocked to the English courses at the British Council. I went along for the induction meeting and saw a few familiar faces as well as many new ones. I felt out of place and self-conscious, and realised how solitary and introverted my life had become. The teaching course was interesting and was a great boost to my confidence, which had been eroded so badly. I'd lost touch with ordinary people and everyday life, and I felt the course was bringing me back to normal life. I'd become very insular and had been drinking too much, a habit I didn't like and wanted to break. It had been a retreat from feeling trapped and stifled but now I wanted it to stop. I threw myself into my homework and the course. I loved the varied schedule, in which we sometimes taught a class for an hour to practise what we learnt. It was very rewarding and I loved meeting the students from all over the world.

I wrote to Dalal to tell her all about it. In her latest letter to me, she'd written:

Dear Pauline,

We have just come back from England and I found it very exciting, it being my first time. Adnan took me to Manchester where he studied and visited his university and the house where he lived as a student. It had all changed, so he said, and found his lodgings had been pulled down and a new development erected.

I went to a specialist to see about my thyroid because I am fed up with taking a pill every day and want to be free from all these chemicals. I have decided to have an operation but it would be more expensive in England, so I have decided to have it in Russia. They assured me that they had done a lot of operations like mine and it wouldn't cost as much.

We bought a lot of clothes and my daughter wanted to buy the whole shop. She loved the fashion and was surprised at their prices, things we can't get in Russia or Iraq for that matter. I don't want to say how many suitcases we had between us but I can tell you they were many. We loved London and went to a nightclub, just the two of us. Adnan was flirting with a lot of girls and I had a few men looking at me. It was a boost to my morale!

By the time you receive my letter I will have already had my operation.

All my love, Dalal.

As I sat at the table doing my homework that evening, the phone rang. By then I hated the sound of the telephone – it always seemed to mean bad news and you could never be sure who was listening in to the conversation. I lifted the receiver but there was no one there. Munem came in from work and poured us two glasses of Scotch.

'What's the occasion?' I asked.

'I don't want to tell you this, but I must,' he said, looking suddenly grim.

'Munem, what is it? Please don't leave me in suspense.'

'It's Dalal.' He said. 'She's dead.' He poured me another glass and I gulped it down, desperately wanting it to dull this sharp and sudden pain I was feeling. This just couldn't be true; her letter had been so optimistic. What could possibly have gone wrong?

'Her body will be arriving in Baghdad tomorrow. I'll go to the airport. You don't need to be there. Just go to their house after you finish your classes.' Dalal had died in intensive care immediately after her surgery. Her kidneys had failed and she could not be revived.

I went to class the next day, with my eyes swollen from crying and wearing black mourning clothes. My friends there and my tutor were sympathetic but no one had the words to make me feel any better. I went to Dalal's home later and hugged her husband and her children. One of her relatives said she didn't think Dalal had been happy in Moscow, but I took out the letter I'd just received and, when they read it, they seemed to feel reassured. I think it helped them to know that Dalal had been happy and thinking positively about her future. She'd never have known a thing after the anaesthetic took hold. I sat down next to her coffin and thought of all the things we'd shared, the laughter and the memories. We were both only 39, surely far too young to die. I'd intended to wear black only for the 40-day mourning period for Dalal but by the time that was over, the black clothes had become a habit, reflecting the mood I was in for much of the time. Many people frowned on wearing black as if you were in permanent mourning; they were superstitious and said it was bad luck because it would only mean one thing: I was inviting Death to visit again.

*

On July 16, 1979, President Ahmed Hassan Bakr appeared on Iraqi television to announce that he was stepping down and handing over power to his deputy, the Vice-President Saddam Hussein, who he described as the man who was best qualified to lead Iraq:

> *For a long time, I have been talking to my Comrades in the [Revolutionary] Command [Council], particularly cherished Comrade Saddam Hussein, about my health, which no longer allows me to shoulder the responsibilities*

with which the Command has honoured me. My health has recently reached the stage where I could no longer assume responsibility in a manner that satisfies my conscience...

While the President's announcement came out of the blue, no one had seriously believed that he would hang on for much longer, with his deputy clearly so eager to take over from him. Also, it was widely known that the President had had various health problems over the years. Saddam Hussein had spent a long time laying the groundwork for his ascent to the very top of political life in Iraq. For years, he'd been taking an increasingly prominent role as the public face of the Iraqi government, both at home and abroad, consigning Bakr to being little more than a figure-head in many ways. Some Iraqis speculated that Saddam could see his position being undermined by the proposed union with Syria which was being discussed in 1979 and decided that it was time for Bakr to go.

Saddam himself had overseen the negotiations between the two Baathist-governed countries to form a loose federa-tion, an idea that had arisen in part to counter the regional power shift after Egypt became the first Arab country to sign a peace treaty with Israel in 1978 – something deplored by both Syria and Iraq. But it emerged that Saddam had deep reservations about the proposed union with Damascus, espe-cially when President Bakr and the Syrian President, Hafez

Assad, agreed on the division of leadership roles. The Iraqi leader would head the new federation with Assad as his deputy. Saddam would be relegated to third in line. Under such a scheme, if President Bakr's health worsened and he wasn't able to govern, the Syrian leader would be his natural successor – not Saddam Hussein, who clearly would not have been Assad's own choice as deputy. Saddam could never have allowed such a plan to carry on to its logical conclusion. With President Bakr now out of the way, Saddam consolidated his own position by launching a purge within the Baath party.

Just days after Saddam was inaugurated, he presided over a meeting of many hundreds of senior Baath officials from all over Iraq. Like many others in Iraq, I followed the proceedings on TV. As I watched the camera pan across the faces in the large auditorium, I recognised many of the people there, including a number of friends of ours. But this was to be no ordinary party conference. As Saddam looked on and puffed his cigar, his new vice-president, Taha Yassin Ramadan, announced that a plot had been discovered and that the conspirators were in that very conference hall and would now be exposed as traitors. Saddam himself then addressed the astonished gathering and spoke of a conspiracy against him and the nation. He stepped aside so that the former secretary-general of the Revolutionary Command, Muhie Abdul Hussein Mashhadi – who had only recently been sacked by Saddam – could come to the podium and give a lengthy detailed account of this supposed plot, in which he said he'd been involved.

A list was read out of people who were told to leave the hall. Dozens were forcibly removed by security men and led away one by one. When one of the men tried to protest, Saddam simply shouted him down, then resumed puffing nonchalantly on his cigar. Astonishingly, several members of the governing Revolutionary Command Council – the governing elite – were among those led out of the hall, including Adnan Hamdani, who only a few days earlier had been appointed deputy prime minister and the head of the presidential office. The party members began to look increasingly uncomfortable: who among them was going to be next? No one knew what specific evidence there'd been and whether it was real or concocted. And if such evidence was fabricated, how could you defend yourself if the new regime was determined to get rid of you? The former Oil Minister, Murtada al-Hadithi, was taken away by the security guards, as was our close friend, Ghazi Ayoub. Ghazi's wife said later that the security guards had even taken his wages from his pockets as they led him away. She never saw her husband alive again but she did discover his fate in the most cruel way. Her doorbell rang one evening but when she opened the door there was no one there; all that had been left was a length of rolled-up carpet. She bent down and pulled the carpet to examine it. Inside, she found her husband's bullet-riddled body. I saw her once after Ghazi's death. We spoke only briefly; she told me she didn't want to cause me any problems so it was best for me if I wasn't seen associating with her.

Sadly, that cruel experience was not unique. I heard of another woman who was summoned to Abu Ghraib prison to visit her husband, who was being detained there. Relieved that she would finally be able to speak to him, the woman rushed to the prison near Baghdad. There, she was led into a room, where she was told she would be able to see him at last. The lid of a large freezer compartment was pulled open just in front of where she stood waiting expectantly – and inside it was her husband's body.

After rapid trials in front of a special court, some of the most senior Baathists, including many members of the Revolutionary Command Council, were executed. Some estimates say that hundreds of people were killed in the purge. Many, many more were imprisoned. The true number of deaths, disappearances and imprisonments will probably never be known. Saddam's retribution had been swift and it had left few Iraqis in any doubt that their new president's hold on power was now seemingly beyond being challenged even by members of his own party and those nearest to him in government – least of all the ones left in the auditorium who'd given him a standing ovation after the so-called 'traitors' were removed. The black-and-white television pictures were shown all over the world. But did anyone realise at that point that this was the shape of things to come for Iraq?

*

Closer to home, my mother-in-law's health had deteriorated and she had another heart attack. We all visited her in hospital and it was clear that this time she would not recover. She died peacefully and her body was taken home to be prepared for burial in the traditional way. Her eldest daughter, Khania, was supposed to help the woman who came to lay out the body but she couldn't face the task so I helped to wrap Bedria in her burial shroud and sprinkle rose-water over her. It was the final thing I'd ever do for a woman who'd once been a foe but who, with the passage of time, I'd come to understand and care about. Sadly, I'd become used to the pattern of family funerals over the years; we seemed to have had more than our share.

The new term for the English-language classes at the British Council was about to start and I was excited about my first teaching assignment. I'd have a late evening class, mainly foreign businessmen who were working on contract for the Iraqi government. Munem was worried about me coming home late; we were all so much more security-conscious these days and I never went out on my own after dark. So, at his insistence, I swapped to a class that started at 6 p.m. I'd be teaching young students, some of them Iraqis, but also others from elsewhere in the Arab world and from the Far East.

I enjoyed teaching; I worked hard and I got a lot out of it. But my happiness there was to be short-lived. Munem informed me that his boss, the Minister of Oil, Tayeh Abdul Karim, had quizzed him about what I was doing at the British Council. Some of the employees of the ministry were doing courses there and must have mentioned that they'd seen me. The minister made it clear to Munem that he deemed it inappropriate that I should be teaching English at the British Council. There was to be no more discussion about it and no explanation. My husband was following orders and now I was expected to follow them too.

I wondered whether the minister suspected that the wife of his deputy and some-time acting minister was in a position where she could potentially cause problems regarding commercially and politically sensitive information. That was clearly ludicrous – as if Munem would discuss the details of confidential energy contracts with me, and I would then memorise them all and discuss them at length with my students in class the next day! Or perhaps Munem himself was starting to see me as a liability and didn't want his career jeopardised in any way? I had no choice; I left at the end of the term. I felt as if most of my life in Iraq had been a struggle; I'd been ground down and could not fight any more. I was being thwarted at every turn. Now what?

I'd hit another dead end, it seemed, and to add to those frustrations, my health began to suffer. My periods became irregular and the hormone injections that my doctor gave me only made me feel worse – moody, tearful and bloated. Munem came up with a solution: 'Go home to England for a month and sort yourself out.' I was very relieved and didn't hesitate for a moment. I was longing to have a break and it would also be a chance to lay the groundwork for our future as a family. Munem and I agreed that now would be the perfect time to start making tentative plans for a life beyond Iraq and his work there. He wanted to establish a bolt-hole: 'It's time we bought a house in England. It would make a good retreat,' he told me. Many of our friends had done the same thing, either returned to England permanently or set up a base there. Iraq no longer held the rosy future they had once sought. Given my British connections, it made perfect sense for us to put down roots there as well.

Munem also wanted me to reserve a place for Mazin at Leeds University. Our son was of an age now when he would really benefit from a good British university educa-tion, just as his father had done. It was the country of his birth, after all, but Mazin hadn't lived there since he was three years old so it would also be a good way for him to get back in touch with his British background. For the first time in I don't know how long I was actually excited about something – and now I could finally see a future for us all away from Iraq. Munem, too, acknowledged that now was the time to be putting down the foundations there for a new life, beyond our insular Baghdad world. He'd seen many of his friends and colleagues and their relatives suffer under Saddam – imprisoned or executed, or they had simply disappeared. I think he'd come to realise that the situation in Iraq was not going to improve and he wanted us all to be free of it. The first step would be taking our son and daughter to England.

This would be my first trip back to England since my mother had died four years earlier. It did not feel the same at all – I had nowhere to call 'home' – but this time I had a purpose, a mission to accomplish. I spent a few days in west London with a close friend of Munem's – Salem and his family had left Iraq for good and were settled in England. Munem had sent money for me and I collected it from Salem. To celebrate my return and give me a bit of a psychological boost, I bought a smart, navy-blue suit and had my hair done. I had a lot to accomplish in a month, but now I felt ready for anything. My next stop would be Leeds, where I had an appointment to see the dean of the university. I'd met him at a conference in Baghdad and mentioned that we'd hoped to send Maz there, so I was now looking forward to setting that plan in motion.

The train to Leeds was already crowded before it had even left London and I struggled to find a seat and somewhere to put my suitcase. A nice young man helped me out and, as we got talking, I noticed his accent. He told me he was Egyptian and was going back to Leeds, where he was studying mechanical engineering. We laughed at the coincidence of my visit to Leeds to reserve a place for my son on the same course. Over the next few hours we talked a lot and I discovered that his uncle was a famous Egyptian actor, Imad Hamdi, who I'd seen countless times in films on Iraqi television. It was good to be able to relax and talk so freely without worrying about what I said or who was listening. When we arrived in Leeds, I was sorry to say goodbye to this young man but hoped that he'd be the kind of friend that Mazin would make when he did come here.

I was staying with Iraqi friends of ours who'd moved to Leeds, where the husband, Ali, was doing his doctorate in civil engineering. I liked the look of the university; it was impressive and I felt Mazin would do very well there. I kept my appointment with the dean and enrolled my son to start in the new term. My next stop was up near Halifax to see my cousin, Sheila. I told her of my plans to build a house and she showed me a choice plot nearby. It was ideal and we agreed on a joint building project, with a house each, side by side. We caught up on the family news and I was shocked to hear that her younger sister, Rita, who was 44, had been very ill. She'd had a partial mastectomy after breast cancer had been diagnosed, but now it seemed the cancer had spread. I'd been close to Rita when we were growing up and I wanted to see her again. I had about two weeks before I had to return to Iraq and it would be good to spend them with Rita down on the coast in Brighton, where she was now living.

Those two weeks turned into two years. On September 22, 1980, Iraqi fighter jets launched a series of pre-emptive strikes on Iranian air bases and Iraqi troops invaded areas of Iran. Saddam seemed to believe that the fledgling leadership of Ayatollah Khomeini – who had swept to power in the Islamic revolution the previous year – would crumble under the pressure and that the War would soon be over. After initially being caught by surprise, the Iranians retaliated. For the next eight years the two neighbours waged a conflict that would have unimaginable consequences for both sides.

Iraq was now a country at war and the borders were closed: it was impossible for me to return, or for my husband and children to leave. I was stranded in England and could barely take in the enormity of what was happening. No one could predict how long the conflict would last, or when the borders would re-open. So I had to think fast; I needed a home and a job. I decided to stay in Brighton – Rita was there and it was a nice town. I got a full-time job in a nursing home; it was demanding but I needed something to pour my energy into, to prevent myself from constantly worrying about what was happening in Iraq. I bought a one-bedroom basement flat for £16,000 so that Munem, Maz and Nada could write to me there or phone any time. It wouldn't be easy for them; the phone lines were routinely tapped by the Iraqi authorities and mail was opened so they'd have to be careful about what they said.

I felt the children would still be safe, though, despite the War. Maz was busy with his university course and Nada was in her last term at secondary school, preparing for her important Baccalaureate exams. When Munem wasn't working, they'd be at home with him; when he was away, they'd stay with his family. He phoned me to say that he had to go to Czechoslovakia on business and would be taking Nada with him. They'd be there for Christmas and wanted me to join them. I was overjoyed at the prospect and couldn't wait to get there. Nada was happy to see me and even Munem seemed to have missed me. We spent a wonderful week together in Prague, a beautiful city that Nada and I explored together while Munem worked long hours. He'd join us back at the hotel in the evenings.

Our time together was over too soon and it was so hard to say goodbye. Nada was fifteen and I felt she needed her mother and I wanted her to come back with me, but Munem insisted she'd be better off with his family until she finished her education. I reluctantly went back to Brighton, resenting the circumstances that were keeping us apart, and they returned to Baghdad. Soon after I arrived home, Munem phoned to see if I'd got back safely. I was touched when he seemed worried that I'd arrived back at my flat later than he'd expected. When I broached the subject of returning to Iraq, he brushed it off, saying the time wasn't right. The time for what? Perhaps he needed time to decide whether he wanted me back or to give the children time to get used to being without me. He and I had been together for 25 years – how much more time did he need?

For the next year, I saw Munem only intermittently. He visited briefly when he was travelling on business and was able to stop off for a few days in England. But I longed to see Mazin and Nada again. Munem eventually summoned me back to Baghdad with a phone call. Nada, he said, had taken a drugs overdose; she had recovered but she needed me there with her. What could possibly have pushed my teenage daughter to the brink of suicide? Would anything like this have happened if I'd been able to be with her all this time? I seriously doubted it. The most important thing was that she was fine now but I could waste no time in getting back to be with her. I organised my affairs as quickly as I could. The house I'd had built next to Sheila's was finished now. It was large and lovely, and would have made the perfect home for me and Munem and our children. I arranged to rent it out but decided to keep my flat in Brighton. It would be a good base when I returned, hopefully with my children. I resigned from my job and began packing. I bought the latest music albums and had recorded lots of videotapes of TV programmes I thought Mazin and Nada would enjoy. I crammed my cases with gifts for them. I said my final, sad goodbyes to my cancer-stricken cousin, Rita, not sure if I would ever see her alive again. Then I locked the door of my flat behind me and headed for London and the flight to Iraq. At long last, I was Baghdad-bound.

13. Inside a Brutal Regime

I awoke as the plane approached Baghdad. It had been twenty years since that first nervous touch-down in Iraq and there'd been many more since then. It felt like a lifetime ago. The modern new international airport – predictably enough named in honour of Saddam Hussein – was full of people but the only ones I wanted to see were my son and daughter. Words couldn't express what it meant to see them again; the only thing better would have been to have had them safely back in England with me. Mazin was 23 now, a handsome young man in his army officer's uniform. He'd graduated with a Bachelor of Science degree and was now serving in the tank regiment in the Iraqi army. He walked up and gave me a manly hug. I'd missed him so much and been so worried about him being in the army at a time of war. The one consolation was knowing that at least he couldn't be sent to the front-line under Iraqi military regulations because he had a foreign-born parent.

Nada was sixteen and blossoming into a beautiful young woman. She'd had a hard year with the family, being constantly bullied into studying hard. She'd done her best but she'd buckled under the pressures and their bullying. They'd been very hard on her and couldn't seem to see that she was struggling to meet their absurdly high expectations. The overdose had been her cry for help but clearly they hadn't been listening. She would have to re-take her exams that year to prepare for the all-important Baccalaureate next year, an international qualification that would help her, whether or not she decided to go to university. I would make sure she had a lot more options than many young Iraqi women, who, if they didn't have a degree and didn't get a good job, could well have their families decide to marry them off to the first man who proposed.

Munem's official car had been despatched to pick me up and, as it approached the gate to our driveway, I marvelled at how tall the date-palms in our garden had grown in the past two years. I wondered what else had changed here. Munem's driver, Towfiq, carried my bags into the house. It seemed he was never far from Munem's side. I always used to say that he spent more time with my husband than I did. The house was very clean and tidy; Munem's sisters had obviously been in to see to all of that. I noticed immediately that all of the old furniture had been replaced in the sitting-room with a new lounge suite and a large square glass coffee table. I liked the look of it, modern and sophisticated. I looked around and all of the many mementoes of Munem's overseas trips were still on display. These were the souvenirs of the long absences that his job had demanded – carpets from Iran, jade ornaments from China, a samovar from the Soviet Union, crystal from Czechoslovakia, jewellery from Mexico and Brazil. There were dozens of objects from all over the world; our house had become a monument to his travels.

Little had changed in the kitchen. I opened the cupboards to find all my crockery and cutlery still in place. Everything was spotless including the non-stick pans which my sister-in-law Khania had scrubbed down with steel-wool scourers until the metal surface shone. It must have taken her ages; she hadn't realised that the black protective non-stick coating was supposed to be that colour. She'd thought they were blackened and dirty from cooking. I noticed that the fridge had been moved from the kitchen to the utility room next door. I opened it and saw that it was full of food. One of Munem's sisters had also been over to prepare a meal for us; she'd left cooked meat in the fridge and all I needed to do was add vegetables and rice to make dinner. I was surprised and touched by their thoughtfulness in getting the house ready for my return. Was it possible that even they had missed me just a bit, I wondered.

While I'd been away, the curtains in the kitchen had been taken down and my favourite Syrian-made embroidered tablecloth was nowhere to be seen. I found them in a storage cupboard and, once I'd replaced the curtains and the tablecloth, it felt as if I was back in my old kitchen again. Mazin's poster of a beautiful seascape was still on the kitchen wall; I always loved to see it because it livened up the walls and made me instantly think of relaxing holidays and beautiful beaches. I looked around this room in which I'd spent so much time. Over the years, it had seen so many family meals, so many cups of tea and heart-to-heart talks with close friends like Dalal. I reached over and turned on the radio; it was still tuned to the BBC World Service as it had always been before I left.

That night, it felt a little strange to be back in my own bed next to Munem when just that morning, I'd woken up in my Brighton flat – a home that circumstances had forced me to create. Now, back in our family home, I watched him sleep and thought how we'd become more like strangers than a couple who'd been together for 25 years. It felt almost like seeing someone for the first time, someone you didn't recognise at all. Eventually, weariness overtook me and I slept so soundly that I didn't even hear Munem get up and leave for work. When I woke up and saw that he'd gone I had a twinge of guilt that I hadn't got up and made his breakfast for him. I turned over and went back to sleep. I dreamed that my mother and I were together again in Halifax; I was so happy to be with her, the children were with us and life was good again. I woke up with a jolt, half-believing the dream was reality and then as I looked around, realising it was not. It was time to get up, time to see what lay in store for me.

It was Friday, and both Nada and Mazin were at home with me. Nada and I sat in the sun on a garden bench that Mazin had made. I was so proud of my son and his accomplishments. I showed them all the music and films I'd brought back for them. We watched the American TV series *Roots* and were moved to tears by the terrible suffering and injustice inflicted in the name of slavery. But the series did show that human beings are capable of rising above the worst miseries that are inflicted upon them. It was a message that wasn't lost on us in a country at war with its neighbour.

I went off to buy groceries, just as I'd had done on countless occasions in the same shops in the same Palestine Road. As I unloaded them at home, Maz came out of the kitchen and took them off me. He was such a kind and thoughtful young man, chivalrous and gentle. He carried the groceries inside; it was such an everyday act but one that meant so much to me, just to have him here with me, doing ordinary things that it had been impossible for me to do with my children for the past two years.

Over the next few days the neighbours all came to visit, including Lesley, my friend who worked at the British Council. We talked about my time in England and the political situation back here in Iraq and I confided in Lesley about my fears for my children's futures if they stayed in Iraq. I wanted to make sure that Nada got the necessary papers to become a British citizen but I wasn't sure how to go about it. I knew that the British embassy in Baghdad was under heavy guard by Iraqi soldiers and I didn't know whether I'd have a problem getting through the security cordon, let alone obtaining the essential paperwork for Nada. I also had nagging worries that Munem would disapprove or think I was up to something but I felt the least I could do was to get Nada's right to British citizenship recognised so that she'd have that option open to her. Lesley was very supportive and said she'd come to the embassy with me. With Nada's and my birth certificates safe in my bag, we set off.

Security was tight outside the embassy compound and our bags were searched thoroughly. The Iraqi soldiers then insisted on frisking us; mercifully, they didn't make us remove any of our clothing but they laughed at our discomfort and embarrassment as they ran their hands repeatedly all over our bodies. They clearly enjoyed having that power over us, knowing we couldn't object to the way they were groping us for supposed security reasons. It was clearly a psychological ploy to put us off returning. There'd always been a security presence outside important foreign embassies but never to this degree, or using tactics like this. I felt that their behaviour showed how the culture was changing – from one of mutual respect to one of intimidation for the sake of it. Trust, it seemed, was a thing of the past. I was so grateful to Lesley for being there with me. I don't think I'd have had the courage to go through that by myself. But I wasn't going to let my own fear jeopardise Nada's chance of a British passport. Inside the embassy, I handed in the paperwork and was told it would take 'some time' to process. 'I'll be back,' I told the official, and I meant it. I was certain that Mazin would have an easier time getting into Britain – he was born there, after all, but I had to make sure there'd be no problems for Nada in the future.

While I was fretting about my children, Mazin too was worrying about me. He arrived home one afternoon with the most beautiful Alsatian puppy. She trotted along happily beside him on a lead as he came to join me on the garden bench, where I'd been enjoying the afternoon sun. He said he'd bought her from a company that was closing down and leaving Iraq. Foreign firms usually had guard dogs as added security in their compounds and many of their workers kept dogs at home for the same reason. 'You need company and protection now that I'm in the Army and Nada's with the family in Karradah so much of the time.' I was so touched by his thoughtfulness; I hated to think of my children worrying about me – I was much more concerned about their safety than my own.

'So, what shall we call her?' I said, leaning down to stroke her glossy coat. She barely even noticed me and only had eyes for Maz as he played with her on the lawn.

We agreed on Kizzy – the name that the hero of *Roots*, Kunta Kinte, had given his baby daughter. We'd just been watching a poignant scene in the series when he'd lifted the baby up towards the sky and named her Kizzy, which meant in his language, 'she who will stay'. We thought it was appropriate for our new arrival. Kizzy became a much-loved addition to the family; she was good company for me and very protective but the moment she saw Maz I'd be forgotten. She was completely devoted to him and followed him everywhere when he was home. Although she was the perfect pet, Kizzy was also capable of rare lapses when left alone in the house while we were all out. When I got back one day, I saw immediately how she had spent her time: bored and frustrated at being without our company, Kizzy had shredded the upholstery of the old couch in the dining room. She'd made such a good job of it that only the wooden frame and a few loose tatters remained. Mazin had to take it away to get it re-upholstered.

Munem was so busy and preoccupied with work that he didn't even notice the couch wasn't there. He came home late at night, too tired to see that anything was amiss. He'd get up very early for work and simply went from the bedroom to the bathroom to the kitchen for a quick breakfast, then out the kitchen door to where his driver was waiting. He didn't seem to even have the time to look anywhere beyond where he absolutely needed to be. But just this once, Munem's blind devotion to his job had worked in our favour and we were able to keep the secret of Kizzy's wild time with the upholstery.

I hadn't been back long before I began to realise how many of our old friends had left Iraq in the time that I'd been away. I could understand why. The country was in a state of war and Saddam's stranglehold on power showed no sign of diminishing. One night, Munem came home from work, ashen-faced and silent. I thought he must have been feeling quite ill – and he was, but not because he was sickening for something. After he'd had a chance to gather his thoughts, he began to tell me falteringly what had happened at work. Munem had been at a top-level meeting with Saddam and members of the Cabinet. It was a low point during the war with Iran and, while ministers were expected to always agree with everything their great leader said and did, they were also expected to come up with solutions to any and every problem, no matter how difficult. The health minister, Riyadh Ibrahim, apparently spoke up and put forward a suggestion that he felt could lead to an honourable way out of the War, without more years of bloodshed, especially when Iraq was by no means assured of victory against Iran. But his suggestion was a radical one and, in retrospect, it seems very foolhardy indeed to have voiced it. He advised that Saddam should step down temporarily and let the former President, Ahmed Hassan Bakr, come back to power. Such a move would skilfully avoid the clash of egos that had built up between Saddam and the Iranian leader, Ayatollah Ruhollah Khomeini, and which had made the War into a virtual grudge match between the two men. The mutual dislike of each other partly had its roots in the Iraqi author-ities' decision to deport Ayatollah Khomeini from the Shia holy city of Karbala in southern Iraq in 1978, at the insis-tence of the Shah of Iran.

The health minister reasoned that with Saddam nudged to one side, the two countries could then negotiate a cease-fire agreement. Once there was peace between the warring neighbours, Saddam could again take over the reins of power. That was the bold theory and it seems extraordinary that he could ever have imagined that Saddam would want to discuss it as a possibility – let alone agree to it. After all, Saddam had done everything possible to undermine and sideline Bakr, to whom he was vice-president for years. Saddam apparently didn't show any immediate reaction to this daring suggestion but only politely requested that the minister escort him into an adjoining room for further discussions. Moments after the two men left, a shot rang out. Saddam returned to the cabinet meeting alone, as if nothing had happened. A senior government figure and a relative of the murdered minister, Abd al-Tawab Mullah Huwaysh, later said with some understatement, 'This powerfully concentrated the attention of the other minis-ters, who were unanimous in their insistence that Saddam remain in power.' It was to become one of the many infa-mous incidents showing Saddam's capacity for bloodlust and cruelty. And it sent out an indisputably powerful message to the Baath party government, the military and the Iraqi people: displease Saddam and you will pay, no matter how senior you are in the government, or how lowly you are in society. Disagreeing with Saddam Hussein or his increasingly powerful sons was tantamount to suicide; it meant sentencing oneself to imprisonment or execution, or both. Speaking the truth could, and would, get you killed. Saddam's inner circle knew that to survive they had to protect him from bad news by any means necessary.

The Iraqi government put out a statement labelling the minister of health a traitor and saying that he had been executed for importing medicines which had resulted in the deaths of many Iraqis. It was announced that one of the minister's business associates had supplied the Iraqi military with medicines, including penicillin stocks which were out of date and should never have been used. The toxic supplies were said to have resulted in the deaths of dozens of soldiers. Whatever the real reason, the killing of the health minister showed that those at the very top of the power structure in Iraq could act with impunity and without inhibitions. Nothing and no one, it seemed, was able to stop them.

It was later said that, when the minister's wife asked for his body to be released for burial, it was returned to her – hacked into pieces. I knew now what Munem meant when he once told me that Saddam Hussein was capable of anything. The health minister's shooting was one of the incidents that Munem did discuss with me; he had to tell somebody, to get it out of his system. It had seemed so unreal to him. But for all that he told me, I knew he kept a lot more back and didn't confide in me about many of the other appalling things he heard and saw. He seemed to have the weight of the world on his shoulders at times and I could see it was taking a toll on him, emotionally and physically. He spent a week at home in bed with the flu once but it seemed more like mental and physical exhaustion. He still tried to keep up with his work, even though he felt absolutely dreadful. His driver, Towfiq, would come every day with his paperwork.

More often than not, Munem would not tell me what was on his mind. Perhaps it was easier for him to try to stay silent; expressing his fears out loud might have just made them even more real. But I knew that when he'd go out drinking heavily with his friends, that some of his worries would come to the surface. It wasn't wise to criticise anything to do with the government and especially not to criticise Saddam himself and no amount of drink could ever be used as an excuse if word got out that you'd said something disloyal. It was a source of real pain for Munem, seeing what the Iraqi leadership was capable of, and how it had deteriorated over the years. He had such a strong commitment to his country. I'd never met anyone who was as committed as he was. He truly believed in the importance of making Iraq a better place; it was like a sacred mission for him and he never lost that desire to do his very best for his country. But over the years, he became disillusioned, not about Iraq's amazing potential but about the Baath party government's ability to govern and to fulfil its responsibilities to its own people.

There was a clear feeling that this was a society under siege, both from an outside enemy and from within. You didn't have to look far to find grim indications of this wherever you looked. One night, Munem and I and two friends were on our way home after an evening out when the car headlights picked up a large object on the road. As we drove towards it, we made the grim discovery that it was the naked body of a man that had been dumped in the deserted street. We were too scared to stop but immediately behind us there was an unmarked bus, the only other vehicle around, and it seemed to have been despatched to pick up the body. We drove on, wondering what Iraq had come to, that bodies could be dumped unceremoniously in the street and then spirited away under cover of darkness. I wondered whether there was a family somewhere in Baghdad worrying about a loved one who had not come home that night and would never again return to them.

On the few occasions that we socialised now, it was usually with Iraqi friends that Munem had made through his work. Inevitably, I felt excluded and like an outsider when we were with them and their wives. They didn't seem to make me feel especially welcome and I got the impression that they rather resented my intrusion into their cosy social life. When we went to clubs, there was even more drinking than usual and whenever a high-ranking government person came in, everyone would stop talking and applaud gratuitously. People didn't even seem to want to dance any more and the conversation was very trivial – everyone seemed too scared to say anything significant or controversial because you never knew who was listening and ready to report back to someone in power. It was impossible to relax in case you let your guard down, or to trust anyone in case you said something that could be considered indiscreet or dangerous. Informers were everywhere, listening for any indication, however innocent, that one's devotion to Saddam Hussein and the government might not be total.

The arguments erupted between Munem and me again and they were only made worse when we'd had a drink. Having a drink, several drinks, seemed to help Munem blot out, for a short while at least, a lot of what happened at work. But it wasn't doing me any good. I reached a point where I didn't even want to go out any more. I became more and more isolated. I realised quite quickly that I was followed wherever I went; there always seemed to be two people stationed near our front gate, who made no secret of the fact that they were watching my movements. Boys on bicycles would routinely follow me when I was out shopping, watching where I was going and who I was talking to. They didn't even try to look inconspicuous. I knew they'd report on me without hesitation if they saw anything they thought was suspicious. They were used widely by the Baath party, who would tell them they were only doing their patriotic duty. Other people had the same experience – it had become commonplace to have this level of surveillance in your everyday life. The informers often passed information to the authorities that was patently untrue and they were simply retaliating for old arguments or disagreements among families, neighbours or colleagues. You didn't even have to do anything to arouse suspicion. It just became part of the increasingly disturbing routine of living here.

In those circumstances, it was reassuring to have our dog Kizzy around, especially when I was out in the car or in the street. I was challenged one day while shopping in the market, where three officials had set up a collection point for donations of gold for the war effort. The government had launched a campaign urging women to give up their gold jewellery. It is hugely important and symbolic for many Arab women; traditionally, they receive gold necklaces, rings, bracelets or anklets as wedding gifts and, under Islamic law, they keep these gifts even if the marriage ends. At this time, Baath party officials were also making door-to-door collections of gold and there were televised ceremonies, where people would bring in their donations of gold to have them publicly weighed and praised in front of the television cameras. Everyone watched to see who gave the most and who gave the least. I'd never seen these three men before and felt they could have been little more than common criminals setting up a makeshift stall and simply using the government's new campaign as a sophisticated way of stealing. Nothing about daily life in Iraq would have surprised me any more.

As I walked past them with Kizzy at my side, one said gruffly to me, 'We want your gold. Didn't you see on television that everyone is supposed to contribute because of the War?'

'I don't have any gold,' I retorted, wondering how far they were going to push this and whether they'd resort to actually trying to yank my wedding ring from my finger. The more they insisted, the more I said I had nothing to give them. Kizzy sensed my unease and began to growl at the men. They could see that neither I nor my dog were going to give way on this so they demanded to know my address. They obviously thought it would intimidate me but I'd had enough of this. 'Why don't you phone my husband, Abdul Munem Al-Samarraie, the acting minister of oil and ask him about it?' I countered, then turned and strode away, thankful that Kizzy was close beside me.

For weeks at a time, it would be just me at home with Kizzy, my constant and faithful companion. She helped to raise the alarm when I scalded myself severely in an accident in the kitchen. Part of the unit became detached as I bent down to open a drawer and the boiling water from the kettle cascaded over me. It was excruciating but with Kizzy's frantic barking and a neighbour close by, I wasn't without help for long. My neighbour took me to hospital, where the wound was dressed but the healing process was slow and painful. Munem was unsympathetic, dismissing it as a silly accident. He'd become so hardened, so unpredictable. He'd had to develop a very tough shell to stop the pressures of his job subsuming him; he just stopped being able to leave that shell at work and be a loving husband and father when he came home.

That air of toughness was in evidence everywhere now; you could feel it in the streets and at times you could see its effects. I watched in horror from my gate one day as a man whipped his horse into a terrified frenzy; the poor creature was still harnessed to its cart and in its distress, reared away from the man and galloped directly towards me. The weight of the cart threw it off balance and the horse missed me, but careered into my garden wall. It writhed in agony from a broken leg and I ran inside to phone for someone to come and put the horse out of its misery. A large crowd had gathered to watch the horse's death throes. It had served its master faithfully and its life had ended so pitifully. I wept for the horse but what I'd just witnessed seemed so symbolic of the state of the country in which we were living. In that dark moment, I wondered if I would ever leave Iraq alive.

14. A Marked Man

Time passed but little seemed to change as the months dragged on. The war with Iran showed no sign of ending despite major military defeats for Iraq. Many Arab and western countries rushed to prop up Saddam, apparently fearful of the spread of Iranian-inspired fundamentalism under the ayatollahs in Tehran. They seemed to adopt a 'better the devil we know than the one we don't' form of foreign policy and it only served to help the Baath party tighten its grip even further. Such a policy did nothing to hasten the end of the War, but only seemed to prolong it.

One of the few moments of real happiness came when Nada finally finished her studies and came home to me. She passed her Baccalaureate with a good result – 72% – enough to get her into the academy of interior design in Mansour, where we used to live when I first came to Baghdad. It was something she'd set her heart on and I was sure she'd do very well. Her aunties insisted that she go into teaching as they had but she had no interest in that and I was certainly not going to force her. She'd had enough of being bullied when she lived with them. Their idea of discipline was certainly not mine – they'd hit her without a second thought and she came to hate being there. She felt like a prisoner and missed me and her friends. But her aunts had insisted to Munem that she'd never pass her exams and never make anything of herself if she didn't stay there and knuckle down. He gave in to them every time. Her only way out was to pass those exams and then they'd have no reason to keep telling Munem that she should stay with them. To her great relief and mine, her exam pass meant freedom from their overbearing influence.

Soon after Nada had come home to live, her aunty Khania sent one of her sons to visit her. I assumed it was just a quick social call, one cousin to another, but he came bearing a gift of bedcovers and asked her to marry him. I was astonished. I threw him and his gifts out the door and told him never to come back again. My daughter was only sixteen and the last thing she'd be doing was getting married, least of all to a cousin. Marriages between first cousins were common and are permitted within Islam, originally as a means of keeping family inheritances together and on the assumption that cousins may be better suited than a marriage arranged between strangers. It still seemed inappropriate to me, almost primitive to marry your teenager off to a cousin, then they'd have children young and you'd eventually watch your grandchildren do the same thing. Munem's sisters had yet again tried to take matters into their own hands and determine my children's destinies – but I was not going to let that happen ever again.

On one of the rare occasions when we had dinner at home, just the four of us, Munem announced that Nada and I were going to England. 'But what about Mazin?' I said, as our son looked at us both. 'He can go later,' said Munem, 'It's more complicated because of him being in the army now.' Mazin stayed very quiet. He was never one to show his feelings too much, he kept his own counsel. Besides, he would not have argued with his father, even if he'd wanted to come with us. I knew it was useless to argue with Munem if he was so adamant about Mazin staying behind. He wanted to control so many aspects of our son's life. I knew my son had a girl-friend with whom he was in love but Munem had made it very clear that he was against the relationship because the girl's parents were divorced. I thought that was rather hypo-critical of Munem, given his own track record of infidelity.

Then Munem turned to me and said firmly, 'But you cannot tell anyone that you're leaving. Not anyone.' It dawned on me exactly what he was saying. Now I under-stood. This was not going to be just a quick holiday visit, this was something much more than that. Munem wanted the trip arranged quickly and quietly, without any fuss that could lead to gossip or speculation. He was too well-known, and if it got out that he was sending his entire family out of the country, we could all have been in danger. This was his way of trying to protect us while he still could. There was no time to lose. I needed to get Nada's papers back from the British embassy; they'd been there for more than a year and I'd still heard nothing definite about her status. I went down to the embassy and explained that my daughter and I were leaving Iraq. The clerk simply shrugged and said the paperwork hadn't arrived yet. I begged him to check and re-check the files. I went to the British Council to say goodbye to old friends and colleagues. Among them was Margaret Hassan, a lovely Irish-born woman who'd been working there for many years. She'd long since made her home in Iraq after marrying an Iraqi engineer, Tahseen. They were such a nice couple, very happily married, and Margaret had adopted his homeland as her own.

In the days before our departure, Nada and I had to be careful about what we packed. It had to look like a holiday visit. We couldn't risk arousing suspicion among the security staff at the airport by taking too many personal possessions or household goods. I gave my gold jewellery to Mazin; it might help him if he needed to raise money to get away and join us. It was agonising saying our farewells but I knew we'd be together again before too long. My son had tears in his eyes as he kissed and hugged me one more time. I couldn't bear to leave him but I knew I had to for my daughter's sake and for my own sanity. I was certain that when things had settled a bit, Mazin would come to join us. Everyone in Munem's life had, it seemed, benefited from his position in some way or another, except his own son and I was going to make sure that wasn't the case this time. 'If you don't tell your father that you want to see us,' I whispered in Mazin's ear, 'he won't send you. Make sure you tell him. I love you and I'll see you soon.'

As Nada and I passed through airport security, we were searched thoroughly by a female guard. Our suitcases were emptied and every item was inspected. I felt my few pieces of jewellery lying against my skin underneath my clothing, small items but of great sentimental value. As we sat on the plane waiting for take-off, I was surprised to see Margaret Hassan come on board and rush down to where we were sitting. She handed me Nada's papers that had finally been released by the British embassy. I was so grateful to Margaret for her great kindness; it was so typical of her to try to do someone a good turn and she knew how much having those papers meant to me and what benefit they could be to Nada. It was an enormous relief to know now that there'd be no problem at immigration at Heathrow or in keeping Nada in England with me. That day, August 16, 1984, our flight carried only three families to England – me and my daughter; a British woman, Maria, who was going back with her young children to visit her mother, and a relative of Saddam Hussein's, who was travelling with his family. Nada and I slept for much of the way.

At least my daughter and I had a home to go to. Just an hour or so out of London, my flat in Brighton was waiting for us and when I stood on the doorstep and put the key in the lock, I was grateful that Nada was with me. The basement flat was a little worse for wear after being empty for two years. It reeked of damp: the bathroom and kitchen had been flooded after a pane of glass had broken in the small conservatory off the kitchen, letting in rainwater. At least the bedroom and the sitting room were still dry. It took us a long time to clear up the mess in the other two rooms and make the flat a comfortable place to be. Nada hated it there, although she seemed to like Brighton. We enjoyed going to different places together and she enrolled in a language school to improve her English, where she soon made friends.

Nada was very homesick for Baghdad and missed her father and brother and her friends. My daughter and I needed to get to know each other again; we'd had so much time apart that we needed to rebuild our relationship. I felt very protective of her; she'd had a sheltered upbringing in so many ways and I was not sure how she'd cope with what I often thought was the excessive amount of freedom and lack of responsibilities that young people had in Britain. I wanted to make a proper home for us – and Mazin and Munem, who I felt sure would join us when they could – so I sold the flat for the same price I'd paid for it and bought a two-bedroom, two-storey townhouse. I bought Nada a car, a Golf GTI convertible, an older model but rather smart, and I knew she'd love the fact it was a convertible. She enrolled for a two-year secretarial diploma course. At last, it began to feel as if we could actually have a normal life, away from fear and repression.

I treasured every letter from Mazin. They made the separation from him seem a little less painful, even just for a few moments. I longed to hear every detail of his life – how his work was going at the Beiji oil refinery, what he was doing in his spare time, whether he was taking good care of himself and, more than anything, when I'd be able to see him again. At one point, I got my hopes up that we'd be reunited, when he told me that he was planning to go to Italy for a few weeks but his holiday never eventuated:

Dear, dear Mum,

I hope you're keeping okay and in good health. I'd like to thank you very much for the things you sent me. They're very nice.

I'm sorry for this short letter but I shall send you more detailed letters in future. I hope to see you in February when I go to Italy for one month.

Dear Mum, I am very busy in Beiji and Baghdad. I'm working a lot in the garden. I made a table-tennis table and I'm keeping myself busy, more inside the house than outside.

Please tell me about you: what you do, places you go, and keep in touch...

Miss you and I love you,

Mazin xxx

Dear Mum,

How are you doing? I hope you and Nada are in good health and keeping okay. I would like you to know that I miss you very much... All our friends and relatives send their regards.

Dear Mum, please send your recent photos; I sent a couple of photos of me in Beiji, but without a moustache. I don't know if Dad told you or not that I have grown a moustache and some say it looks nice, especially my girlfriends.

I'm okay and don't be [worried] about me. I spend most of the week at work in Beiji as you know and I find it interesting, though sometimes boring because of the bad weather. The weather here in Baghdad is beautiful at this time of the year.

I hope to hear from you very soon. Keep writing. Enjoy your time and keep in touch.

Mazin xxxx

xxx

Munem phoned unexpectedly one day to say he was coming to England for a few days. Nada was thrilled to see her father; she sat next to him and lovingly smoothed back his hair from his forehead. I could see him visibly relax, just being with us. He was proud of how Nada had settled in and that she was about to start her new course. Nada and I were desperate to know when Mazin would be able to join us but

Munem was non-committal: 'I'm working on it,' was all he'd say. I was frightened for Munem; we both knew that anyone in favour with Saddam Hussein one day could fall from grace the next with tragic consequences. So many people had been executed or imprisoned, or had disappeared without trace. I felt certain that Munem may have known that he too could be in danger but he was prepared to take his chances.

After just a couple of days, Munem had to leave; he'd interrupted a business trip to come and see us and now had to get back to his work. We had no idea when we'd be together again. But soon after, Munem did return very briefly and asked me to meet him at a hotel at Heathrow airport, where he'd stopped in transit on a business trip. When I walked into his room, a number of his friends were there with him. All of them had left Iraq for good and were living in England. Munem took me to the other end of the room and sat me down. I wondered what could be so urgent that he had to summon me to a hotel room and didn't have time for a proper visit.

In a quiet voice, he said, 'I've been told by Saddam that I must leave Iraq.'

'But that's all right because you'll come here,' I said, with great relief, because I thought it meant we'd all be reunited.

'But I can't leave. I'm too afraid for Mazin and my family.' There was such sad resignation in his voice that I knew for Munem there was no turning back. He wasn't worried for himself but in fear of retribution: he couldn't bear the thought of anything happening to Mazin or to his own brothers and sisters. A person's love for their family was one of the secret weapons that the government would use against its critics – it was a way to keep them in line, they'd never jeopardise the lives of their loved ones.

I hardly dared ask the question but I had to know. 'Do you mean that Mazin won't be coming here?'

'I'll try,' said Munem, 'I'll try.' The enormity of what he was saying hit me and I could feel all the hopes I'd been cherishing slip slowly but surely from my grasp.

*

I never saw Munem again. I waited for news, for word from him or his family, but there was only silence. I went to his friend, Salem, who told me what had happened after Munem had returned to Iraq. He'd been imprisoned. Salem said my husband had been shown on television, wearing pyjamas, saying that he had worked hard for his country, that he had devoted everything he had to making Iraq a better place. Salem told me that Munem was executed without a trial along with Salem's brother and several others on August 19, 1986. He said that Saddam had demanded of him that he pay $10 million in exchange for his brother's life; Salem told him he could only raise $4 million but that was not good enough for Saddam Hussein. Salem's brother was executed along with the others. Salem gave me a copy of Munem's death certificate, which had been obtained through Amnesty International. My husband was buried in the family plot at Samarra.

I suspect that Munem had spoken out against something that outraged him, some awful deed that he could not keep silent about. People told me that Munem used to talk a lot; eventually, he couldn't keep his thoughts to himself. He knew you had to be totally subservient to Saddam Hussein and the Revolutionary Command Council, and if not, you would pay with your life. Munem had gone back to Iraq for that final time in defiance of Saddam, purely to protect his son. It was tantamount to signing his own death warrant.

15. *I Never Said Goodbye*

As the months went by, Nada and I became increasingly desperate to contact Mazin. We phoned Munem's family's house repeatedly but most of the time, the phone simply rang and rang, and no one even answered. On the rare occasions when we did get through to them, my sisters-in-law would always say that Mazin was out with friends or at work. They were so evasive, it was impossible to get any information out of them. They seemed worried that the phones were bugged and didn't want to say anything that could be used against them. We phoned our house in Baghdad but Mazin was never there either. I wrote to him begging him to get in touch but I was afraid to say what my real fears were because I knew the letter would be opened and read by the authorities, and I didn't want to say anything that could be misconstrued by some official – especially one who may not have a good command of written English – and could cause problems for Mazin.

I didn't know what to do. I couldn't go to Iraq, leaving Nada alone in England, and I couldn't take her back to Baghdad with me – it was too risky. I had no one to turn to and no one I could trust. Just when everything seemed hopeless, I got a letter from Mazin, saying he wanted to join us and asking how he could get a British passport:

31 July, 1987

Dear, dear Mum

How are you, Mum? I hope you're in good health. I'm so sorry for not writing to you because I'm so busy these days. Please, Mum, don't worry about me. I'm fine and miss you so much and am waiting for the day I can see you.

Dear Mum, I was looking for my British birth certificate and couldn't find it, so what I want to say is, could you find a copy or try to get one... With the certificate, I hope [to get] a British passport. If you can't find my birth certificate, I'll have to look again and send it to you. I've enclosed four [passport] photos...

This is the only way I can think of to see you.

I love you,

Mazin xxx

* Consider this matter top secret

It was so typical of Mazin to be more concerned about me than himself but reading between the lines, I could sense his need to get out and I was desperate to help him, to bring him to safety in Britain. It was unbearable to think that he might be stuck in Iraq with no way out. It chilled me to read the last line – 'Consider this matter top secret'. I read it over and over again; what did it mean? Was he in immediate danger? Who was he frightened of? Had he been threatened in some way? I wrote back immediately telling Mazin to take his birth certificate and passport photos to the German embassy in Baghdad, which I'd been told was handling such matters on behalf of the British embassy, which was now closed because of the war with Iran.

I didn't know how best to convey the urgency of the situation to Mazin without arousing suspicion in any official who intercepted the letter. I just hoped he would act on my advice without delay. I went to see Munem's friend, Salem, for his advice on what I should do. He told me to go to Iraq to get Mazin and bring him back. But another friend of Munem's said I risked making things worse if I went. I was in a quandary. Returning to Iraq could mean the end for me and then what would happen to Nada? But if there was any chance of saving Mazin, it would be worth the risk.

Before I could make definite plans, Salem told me he had some terrible news: Mazin had been detained and was being held in Abu Ghraib prison, just west of Baghdad. It had been built by a British contractor in the 1960s and since then, had developed a notorious reputation as an interrogation centre. The prison, which sprawled over 280 acres, was divided into five separate walled compounds housing inmates on long prison terms, others serving short sentences, foreign prisoners, those interred for political crimes and prisoners whose crimes warranted the death penalty. Abu Ghraib was said to hold large numbers of soldiers and officers who opposed the war with Iran, as well as opposition figures and critics of the Baath party. I tried to get information out of Munem's family but they couldn't – or wouldn't – tell me a thing about what was happening with Mazin.

I was being driven mad with worry. But Nada's friend Helana wrote to her and we felt we were getting closer to an explanation. Helana, who lived next to Mazin's one-time friend Hafeth, in our neighbourhood, said Mazin had been followed by a gang of Baathist youths led by Hafeth. She said they were always harassing Mazin and one day he just snapped and challenged them, telling them to leave him alone. He told them he was an officer in the Iraqi army and didn't see why he should put up with harassment and taunts from the likes of them. There'd been an argument, during which he apparently shouted at them, 'Do you want to kill me like you killed my father?' Their response was to report him and have him dragged off to prison.

The months of waiting for information on Mazin stretched agonisingly into years. We could get no official details from the authorities so we had to rely on Munem's family for information. We phoned persistently but it was rare that they actually answered. When we finally did get through, one of Munem's sisters or his youngest brother, Assarm, would simply say that Maz was okay, that they were visiting him in prison and were taking him essential things. They assured us that they were looking after him as best they could and that he'd be released eventually. It was small consolation but I clung to the thought that he was still able to have visits from his aunts and uncles and cousins, and that he knew he had not been abandoned and forgotten.

Nada and I felt as if we too were living in prison – an invisible prison. We couldn't see the bars but we knew they were there, holding us in. The persistent emotional ache that we felt for Mazin and our efforts to find out what was happening became part of our everyday lives, something that was always with us. The war with Iran eventually ended in 1988 but, even as Iraq began returning to something like normal, it didn't prove any easier to get information about Mazin, no matter how hard we tried. Nada and I tried to keep busy and, in 1990, she finished her secretarial course. She decided to stay in Brighton. She wanted and needed security in her life, which I understood after everything she'd been through, which was so much more than other young women she knew. She got married and, although her wedding was lovely, we both knew that it would only have been a truly joyous occasion if her father and brother had been with us. She looked stunning and her father would have been very proud of her. Many old friends we'd known in Iraq, who were now living in Britain, came along and shared the celebrations with Nada and her husband, Haithem. It was good to see everyone again and to have something happy to celebrate for once, even though our sadness for Munem and our fears for Mazin were never far from our minds.

We waited still longer for more news of Mazin but there was nothing from Munem's family. We never gave up phoning, we clung to that chance – however tiny or unlikely – that we'd actually get through to them and hear them say that Mazin was fine, and safe and home with them. I was desperate to hear anything of Mazin and when I answered my doorbell one day, to see Najeeb, a cousin of Munem's, standing there, I felt he must know something. I ushered him inside and as he side-stepped my two beloved Bichon Frise dogs, Samba and Tango, yapping excitedly around him, I insisted on hearing anything he could tell me about Mazin. 'He's still in prison, I think,' said Najeeb, 'but Hashmia doesn't go and see him the way she used to.' He sounded apologetic. 'These days everyone is afraid to ask questions and when they do, they don't get any answers.' That was not what I wanted to hear but at least it was a scrap of information.

'Assarm is in prison, too,' he said, as if it made it any easier to know that Munem's youngest brother had also been carted away. There was no more he could tell me.

Najeeb said he was now living in England and studying in Manchester. I invited him to stay the night, though, and gave him Nada's old room. He was disappointed when I said she was married now and in her own home. He admitted that he'd once hoped that Nada would marry him. I was taken aback by this confession, especially given that he was married himself now. But Nada would be over to visit tomorrow, I said, and he'd have a chance to catch up with her then. Before he left the following day, we talked some more about Mazin and it hurt me to hear him say that the family didn't give Mazin the guidance they should have, after we left and his father was executed. I'd done everything I could for that family and when my son needed their support, they seemed to have given up on him. I cursed Hashmia for not going to visit him any more but as long as one of his other aunties or cousins did still see him in prison whenever they could, I thought, that's at least something.

Mazin's thirty-second birthday was on November 20, 1991. Nada gave birth to her son, whom she named after her brother, three days later. I was with her during the baby's birth, such a wonderful experience to share. Her husband, Haithem, was away in Bahrain for a job interview so he missed his son's birth. They moved to Bahrain and began a new life there. A new chapter opened up for me as well. I decided I needed a complete change and, for the second time in my life, moved to another country, with high hopes for the future. I invested in a petrol station business in Florida, along with a family friend – Mohammed Soboh – and his two brothers. Their family originally came from Palestine but they'd been forced off their land when the state of Israel was created in 1948 – in what the Palestinians call *al-Naqba,* the catastrophe – and had fled to Jordan as refugees. Mohammed's parents had instilled a strong work ethic in him and his brothers. My dream was to get Mazin to the US and hand over my share of the thriving business to him. It was still proving impossible to get calls through to Munem's family but we never stopped trying.

I had virtually no information to go on. But Mohammed had promised me that he'd try to find out what was happening to Mazin. He said it would be a lot easier for him to do that if he went to Iraq from Jordan, the next time he was visiting his family. He had a cousin who was studying medicine in Baghdad so it would not look suspicious if he went there as an ordinary visitor. In 1993, he visited Iraq and I was overjoyed when he phoned me to say that he'd seen Mazin, who'd just been released from prison. Mazin, he said, had been very weak after his ordeal, unable to speak but was recovering at home with Munem's family. At least my son was alive and when he built up his strength, I felt certain he'd be able to travel and join me. But we heard nothing for another two years.

By 1995, it was getting easier to travel to Iraq in the years following the Iraqi invasion of Kuwait and the conflict that followed. My Iraqi passport had long since expired but I would have resisted ever using it anyway, so I applied for an entry visa as a British citizen and, after a fairly long bureaucratic delay, it was granted. By September, we were ready to leave. I went out shopping and stocked up on clothes and gifts for Mazin. I had to guess at the sizes – it had been so long since I'd seen him and he'd been through so much – but I just wanted to spoil him. It had been so many years since I'd actually been able to shop for my son that now I was really enjoying it, trying to guess what colours and styles he'd like, and what would suit him. Shopping was actually a fun experience when I was doing it all with Mazin in mind. We flew to Jordan, where Mohammed's family were waiting to greet me in Amman. There was a minor setback when it was discovered that my luggage hadn't been on the same plane. I was more worried about the prospect of losing all of the things I'd bought for Mazin than of losing any of my own belongings but, fortunately, the following day my bags did turn up.

I'd had a sleepless night but at least I was here in Jordan now and much nearer to seeing Mazin than I'd been in years. Mohammed's brother, Majid – one of the partners in our business – their mother, Umm Jamal and her lawyer brother, Abu Ashraf, would be coming with me. Ostensibly, we'd be going to see Abu Ashraf's son, the young man who was studying medicine at Baghdad University. I felt such a mix of excitement and anticipation, and apprehension that I could barely speak. At last I was about to begin the journey that would end in a reunion with my son. Umm Jamal and her family had done everything possible to help me prepare for the trip. They'd found a driver who had the required special licence to bring passengers into and out of Iraq and they'd stocked up on cigarettes, to be used at regular stages of the trip to bribe guards at the numerous checkpoints we'd encounter along the way. We waited at the border along with a large number of cars, trucks and buses. Every vehicle and its occupants had to be searched. We paid the border crossing fee and were directed to a building where everyone had to give a blood sample. Majid tried to dissuade the doctor from taking blood from Umm Jamal, saying his mother had heart problems and shouldn't have blood taken in this way. When no one was looking, he slipped the doctor $50; the doctor took both the money and the blood sample.

Eventually, it was our turn to go through the security checkpoint. Our vehicle and our belongings were searched and we were all frisked. The whole process seemed to take an age but finally we were able to set off on the long dusty road to Baghdad. We got there in the evening and were staying with the family who were hosting Abu Ashraf's son. They prepared a lovely meal for us but I could barely taste the food, I was so full of anticipation about the prospect of seeing Mazin the next day. I barely slept that night. Early the next morning, I was up and ready to go. It was a beautiful

September day, the best time of year to be here, with a
dazzling blue sky and brilliant sunshine. The heat of the day
was much more bearable now that the summer months and
the heavy dust storms had passed. We drove through neighbourhoods that were so familiar to me, especially the streets
of Karradah, where Munem's family lived and which I'd
driven along countless times over the years.

There had been a few changes. The road to my in-laws'
house was paved now and the orchard that had once grown
so luxuriantly opposite had been levelled and houses had
been built on the land. The new houses made theirs look old
and small by comparison. We pulled up outside their house
and I leapt out of the car, almost running to the front door.
My hands were shaking as I pressed the doorbell. There was
no reply. I banged on the closed metal gate at the side of the
house, thinking they may not have heard the bell. There
wasn't a sound inside. Maybe Mazin was at our old house
and not living here after all? Perhaps he was at work?
Perhaps my sisters-in-law were out shopping? It was only
when I stepped back to look around that I noticed how
neglected the house looked. It barely looked as if anyone
was living here now. The once-lush garden was now a shriv-
elled mass of bare brown and the plants and fruit trees
were all dead. I went to the house next door, wondering if
the same neighbours still lived there. The wife of their
eldest son opened the door to me. We instantly recognised
each other and she seemed shocked to see me, especially

when I asked, 'Muna, where's Mazin?' She looked at me dumbfounded and just shook her head. Muna stepped forward and put her arms around me without saying a word. I shook her off and pulled away, and strode back to the house, where Majid had managed to prise open the heavy metal gate leading to the back of the house. I walked down the path and saw the back door ajar. I ran inside, calling out, 'Mazin! Mazin!'

The house was silent. In the family room at the front, I found Assarm. He'd pulled a sheet over his head and was cowering on the bed. I don't know who or what he was hiding from, but he was clearly a terrified man. 'Assarm, Assarm,' I said, as gently as I could. 'It's me, Pauline.' When he heard my voice, he dropped the sheet from his face and looked at me in astonishment. He hugged me but he was strangely silent and I had to ask the one thing I was desperate to know. 'Assarm, where's Mazin? I need to know.'

I thought for a moment that he hadn't actually heard me. He seemed to be trying to summon up the words but just couldn't get them out. It was obvious he was shocked to see me but his surprise at my unexpected visit didn't explain his behaviour. I stared at him, willing him to tell me where my son was. Nothing mattered more to me right now than just seeing Mazin. I'd come so far, waited so many years, and now all I wanted was a simple answer to my question. Assarm looked up at me and said simply, 'Saddam hanged him.'

Those three words seemed to take an eternity to sink into my consciousness. But when they did, I could feel my body start to shake with each sob, with each gasping 'No, no, no...' All these years I'd been living in hope, believing somehow that my son would be safe. Munem's family knew I thought Mazin was still alive. 'Why didn't someone tell me?' I railed at Assarm. How could they not tell me that my son had been executed? What kind of people were they to be this cruel? What did they hope to achieve by not even telling me or my daughter? I felt utterly betrayed.

'I was put in prison, too,' said Assarm. 'I was tortured and beaten. I didn't know what was going on, or what they were going to do to me in there.' I could see how pitiful Assarm looked; he was only a little older than Mazin and they'd been like brothers when they were growing up. I know Assarm must have suffered in prison but at least he was alive and back in his own home. His sisters had helped him far more than they'd helped Mazin. Assarm told me that he now lived alone in this old house, living a hand-to-mouth existence, surviving on what money he could get from selling the possessions his sisters had stripped from my family home. They'd brought everything back here – my jewellery, the paintings, books, furniture, photographs, the crystal and jade. The house and our belongings were my daughter's legacy and now she'd been denied them.

I was in shock but I was also very confused. I didn't understand this at all. How was it possible that what

Assarm was telling me was true, that Mazin had been executed on July 10, 1988? My friend Mohammed had seen him long after that when he'd gone to Baghdad to try to find Mazin in 1993. He'd come to this very house and sat here, looking at Mazin, worried about how exhausted my son had been. Assarm's sisters had told Mohammed that Mazin had just been released from prison and that's why he looked so ill and was barely able to sit up unaided, let alone able to speak to him. Mohammed had given one of them, Hashmia, $6,000 to look after Mazin and get him everything he needed to restore his health and to make him well enough to be able to join us in England. At that moment it became painfully clear just how Mohammed had been deceived. Assarm had no choice now but to admit it. 'It wasn't Mazin who Mohammed saw,' he said, barely able to look me in the eyes. 'It was me. I didn't know what my sisters had said to him. I was too weak to know what was going on or even to speak.' All this time, they'd lied to us, again and again and again.

I couldn't believe what I was hearing from Assarm; the calculated cruelty, the lying and deception of these women was unspeakable. 'Shall I take you to see them?' he asked. The sisters and their widowed father now all lived in a house belonging to one of the younger ones, Madeha, who was now divorced. Assarm had argued with them over his girlfriend, of whom they didn't approve, and had ordered them all out of the house. He hadn't spoken to them for some time. Now I wanted to see them and I wanted to hear their explanations and excuses. One of the sisters, Emel, arrived at the house just as we were leaving. She did not say hello or hug me, but only walked right past me and argued with Assarm in Arabic because he'd told me about Mazin. 'Why shouldn't he have told me?' I responded, also in Arabic. If I was shaking with excitement when I walked towards this house, I was now shaking with rage as I walked away from it.

With my friends beside me, I went to face the family. The house was full of women and children, apart from my father-in-law. Only he and Madeha had a bedroom each, the others and their children were crammed into one room. My brother-in-law Hashim's wife made tea for me and as she fussed around, I wondered whether she was the family's latest drudge just as I had been so many years ago. Her husband was away working in Yemen so she and her children were living here too. Her attempts at hospitality were meaningless. I was too upset for tea. When the women realised why I was here, they began crying and wailing. My own tears were unstoppable but I was not here for their sympathy; I was here to find out why my daughter and I had been lied to for years. It was a waste of time. There was no explanation and no apology.

Faleha hugged and kissed me, and said that having me here was as if Munem was back among them again. Her husband, Shakir, had at least made an effort to get details about where Mazin's body had been taken and for that I was grateful. An official would give him only a reference number – 519 – and advised him to keep it quiet and not try to pursue it any further. Hashmia, who'd given up on visiting Mazin when he needed it most but had happily taken the money Mohammed had brought with him to help my son, could not face me and didn't appear while I was at the house. That to me was a sure sign of a guilty conscience. I found out that the family had let out our house to a relative and were receiving rent for it. Hashmia had no reason to take our house away from us. Munem had bought her a flat of her own. The greed appalled me and I became convinced that it was a big factor in them keeping Mazin's death a secret. That way, we were kept at bay and wouldn't come back to reclaim our house and our belongings, or sell the place and deprive them of the ready source of income that it had become for them. I left them in disgust, these people who felt like strangers to me now, not in the least like a family who should have done everything they could to help my son, their own nephew. I'd lived in their midst, mourned with them, celebrated with them, shared our lives with them and now they were less than nothing to me.

Later, I sat alone in the bedroom of the house where my friends and I were staying, numb with grief and despair, tears streaming down my face until I fell asleep from sheer emotional exhaustion. Before we left Iraq a few days later, I saw Assarm again and gave him all the clothes I'd lovingly chosen and bought for Mazin in Florida. There was no point in taking them back with me; packing them with Mazin in mind had been such a happy experience but now they were only a sad reminder that my hopes had been crushed. I prepared to leave Baghdad. I didn't have the chance to visit Munem's grave in Samarra and it was impossible at that point to find out where Mazin was buried.

As my friends and I drove through Baghdad, I heard the familiar sound of the President's voice blaring out from a loudspeaker on a street corner; a speech by Saddam was being broadcast and speakers were set up everywhere so you couldn't escape hearing his words. It was uncanny: in 1962, when I'd first arrived in this city, I'd heard another president's voice blaring from loud-speakers in the streets, just as Saddam's was now. I could only hope with every ounce of my being that Saddam too would be overthrown just like President Qassem, whose voice I'd first heard echoing around the streets on my first day in Baghdad more than 30 years earlier. But, as I listened to Saddam's recorded voice fade into the din of the traffic behind me, it barely seemed credible that his vile acts would catch up with him and that he'd be held accountable.

We drove on towards the border with Jordan and I could feel that I was moving further and further away from my old life, my old hopes, my old dreams. As the car reached Jordan, I felt a closure on a part of my life that I hadn't been able to let go of until then. The echoes of the past were with me forever but getting fainter, tucked away safely in a part of my heart with my precious memories. Back in Amman, I said goodbye to the friends who'd done so much for me and helped me achieve what had become a very painful goal. I don't think I'd have had the strength and courage and willpower to have made that journey on my own and, thanks to them, I hadn't had to. I returned to Florida and to work but it didn't feel quite the same any more. I'd once hoped that Mazin would join me here and take over the business but that would never happen now. The heavy workload was a good distraction but it no longer seemed to have a point to it, if I wasn't building up a business to hand over to my son. I'd lost the drive I once had to make it a success.

My health began to falter and it didn't take me long to decide that my real home was in England after all. I missed it so much; it's where my roots are and where I feel happiest. I left Florida on New Year's Eve, 1997. Before the plane took off, the cabin crew served everyone a glass of champagne and we all raised a toast to the New Year and to our private hopes and dreams for the future. Eventually Nada left Bahrain and she too returned to live in England. Her marriage ended and, some years later, she married my loyal friend, Mohammed, and they have two beautiful young children together. Her eldest son, Mazin, is growing into a fine young man. His grandfather and the uncle for whom he was named would have been proud of him. Their deaths brought Nada and me closer together and we support each other in our grief and in our struggle to live for the present, not the past. Nada had returned to Baghdad in 2001 and stayed with her aunt Hashmia but she wasn't able to find out any further information about Mazin's death or where he was buried.

Just as I'd done in my living room in 1958, 45 years later I watched as the television showed scenes of chaos and monumental upheaval in Iraq. I watched as Saddam Hussein's seemingly inviolable grip on power was broken in the United States-led invasion of 2003. I watched as the ubiquitous statues of him all over Iraq were hauled to the ground by angry crowds and tens of thousands of posters and portraits of him were torn to shreds. Schools, colleges, hospitals, public offices, streets and suburbs that were named in his honour were hastily re-named. Saddam Hussein International Airport in Baghdad became simply Baghdad International Airport; the sprawling, densely-populated Baghdad suburb of Saddam City became Sadr City. The Baath party was outlawed, the hated Mukhabarat intelligence service dismantled and the military and police supposedly purged of his supporters. But the legacy of Saddam Hussein will not be so easily removed from history. I watched the television images of the carnage of war and the sectarian blood-letting that have followed in the years since he was ousted.

I saw the photographs of the bodies of Saddam's murderous sons, Uday and Qusay, who were killed when

US forces stormed a house in Mosul in northern Iraq, in July 2003. At last Saddam himself experienced what so many thousands of us had experienced because of him – the agony of losing a son or daughter whom we could not save from the horrors he perpetrated. Months later, I watched the images of the capture of their father. A dishevelled, dirt-smeared Saddam was hauled out of the hole he'd been hiding in, by US troops who found him near his hometown of Tikrit in December that year. He'd been betrayed by an informer lured by the US promise of a multi-million dollar reward. Three years later, the eventual trial of the murderous, egotistical tyrant showed that his luck had at last run out. I used to feel such rage at the thought of Saddam Hussein living in unimaginable opulence, abusing his power with impunity, and with the whole of Iraq at his fingertips, while my husband and son perished, thanks to him. Seeing him emerge from that grimy little hole in the ground and later undergoing physical examinations while television cameras recorded his capture and humiliation for all to see was cold comfort after all that has happened.

I've watched as the bloodshed has continued in Iraq and tens of thousands of innocent lives have been sacrificed. Among them was the gentle, unassuming Margaret Hassan, who'd been so kind in getting Nada's citizenship documents to me just as we were about to leave Baghdad. Margaret was abducted by armed men as she was being driven to work on October 19, 2004. She was just a few hundred yards from the office where she worked as the national director of the Iraqi branch of the aid agency, CARE International. Her kidnappers released videos of a distraught Margaret pleading for her life and the release of women prisoners in Iraq. She urged the British people to put pressure on the Prime Minister, Tony Blair, to withdraw British troops. That issue, she said, was why she and other foreigners were being taken hostage. This was a woman who'd done nothing but work for the good of the Iraqi people.

It was a mark of the respect in which she was held by many Iraqis that there were vocal protests in Baghdad demanding her immediate release, and several prominent insurgent groups condemned her kidnapping and urged her captors to free her. Margaret had made their country her home for more than 30 years and for 14 of those years, working for CARE International, she'd helped them in countless ways, not least setting up water treatment projects, health care and nutrition programmes, and trying to ease the suffering caused by Saddam's mis-rule and years of international sanctions on Iraq. She could easily have left the Iraqi people to their fate and saved herself, returning to a comfortable, safe life in her birthplace, Ireland, or to Britain, where she'd spent her childhood. But unlike so many others, Margaret Hassan and her husband Tahseen decided to stay in Iraq.

The last video released by her kidnappers 20 days after she was abducted, showed them brutally executing Margaret with a bullet to the head. She paid for her courage and her commitment with her life. Two years after her murder, three men appeared in a Baghdad court charged with aiding and abetting Margaret's abduction. Only one was convicted and sentenced to life imprisonment. Her loyal family were outraged and have vowed to get to the truth of what happened and why. They feel that the system has failed them and their sister, and they say they're appalled at what they believe was the British government's mishandling of the situation from the very beginning. They too want justice. Margaret's family learned later that her driver was a former officer in the Baath party's security arm, the notorious and much-feared Mukhabarat. Her head of security worked for the Iraqi Air Force during the years Saddam was in power.

Like Margaret, Munem had also refused to leave Iraq and save himself. He wanted to stay so he could protect our son. That proved impossible. It was only after the fall of Baghdad in 2003 that we found out where Mazin was buried. My sister-in-law Faleha's husband, Shakir, could finally use the reference number he'd been given. A search through official records showed that Mazin had been buried in a mass grave near Abu Ghraib prison. We found out that many of the bereaved families had been able to leave markers at the site in memory of their loved ones, who were buried there. It was only one of several mass graves found in the area. Many thousands of executions had been carried out in Abu Ghraib under Saddam's regime so it's unclear just how many people are buried in those mass graves.

After the invasion in 2003, the United States military took over the prison and gave it a more innocuous name – the Baghdad Central Confinement Facility. But Abu Ghraib's brutal legacy lived on in the abuses committed by US soldiers against detainees there, which were revealed in April, 2004. The place seemed cursed. A month later, President George Bush announced that Abu Ghraib would be demolished, an act that he said would be indicative of what he called Iraq's new beginning. The prison, he said, 'became a symbol of disgraceful conduct by a few American troops who dishonoured our country and disregarded our values'. The interim Iraqi authorities, however, seemed to disagree with his decision to have the place torn down and, by mid-June, a US military judge had ruled that the prison constituted a vast crime scene and could not be demolished.

In September, 2006, the prison was closed and the US military returned the abandoned facility to the Iraqi government, after moving the thousands of prisoners to other detention centres. Many Iraqis wanted to see it levelled to the ground rather than stand as an ominous reminder of the horrors that were committed there. In Iraq, Abu Ghraib will always be a byword for brutality. I hope the crimes committed there by Saddam's regime and the institutionalised butchery that took place within its walled compounds will never be forgotten, nor overshadowed in the history books by the actions of a few US soldiers who seemed to claim that they were making Iraq a better place by the ritualised abuse and humiliation of Iraqi detainees. An American Congresswoman, Jane Harman, described those Abu Ghraib incidents as a moral stain on America's efforts in Iraq and on its image around the world. For me, Abu Ghraib will always be a stain on my life – the place where my husband and son were murdered by Saddam Hussein's regime.

I believe we came close to getting Mazin out of Iraq, but not close enough. There are moments of grief and guilt still and those moments will always be with me. I never said a real goodbye, I never had the chance to say 'I love you' one last time. I know that when someone you love dies, it's natural, maybe almost inevitable, to feel guilty that you didn't say enough or do enough. But there is a special kind of grief reserved for parents who out-live their children. There is a part of you that will always say, 'It was never meant to be this way'. The mourning never really ends. There are times when I blame myself and wonder if I could have done more or whether things would have been different if I'd been able to stay in Iraq. At times, I've wished that I'd never left Baghdad but then I have to ask myself, would Nada and I have survived when Munem and Mazin did not? Perhaps we too would have lost our lives. We will never know the pain and suffering that our loved ones endured. We are proud of them and they will never be forgotten. We may never know what might have been, but one day Nada and I will go back to Iraq together and demand justice. We'll insist on our rights to the home and possessions that were taken from us by Munem's family. But the passage of time is taking its toll on them as well – two of his sisters, Khania and Hashmia, died within a week of each other in 2006. Faleha and her husband also suffered the loss of a son when their young boy was killed by a hit-and-run driver as he played just outside their house. It's a loss I would not wish on anyone. Tragedy has left none of us untouched.

I know that one day we will be able to visit Munem's grave in Samarra. One day we will leave a marker stone near Mazin's burial place in memory of our lost boy. Despite all that has happened I still believe there is such a thing as justice. In October, 2006, a special tribunal set up in Baghdad to try Saddam Hussein and some of his cohorts sentenced him to death for the killing of almost 150 Shias in the 1980s. They died during a military clampdown in the aftermath of a failed assassination attempt on Saddam in the town of Dujail in 1982. Within days of that verdict, he was back in the same courtroom in the heavily fortified area of Baghdad known as the Green Zone to face charges of genocide for a military campaign against the large Kurdish community in northern Iraq. It was known in Iraq as Anfal – the 'spoils of war' campaign – and court documents refer to the deaths of tens of thousands of Kurds. Saddam Hussein did not live to hear whether or not the tribunal accepted his version of the bloody events in the Anfal campaign. He was executed in Baghdad at dawn on December 30, 2006, on the first day of Eid al-Adha – the Muslim festival of sacrifice, so named because it commemorates the prophet Abraham's sacrifice of a sheep in the place of his son Ishmael, as commanded by God. I watched the television coverage at my daughter's home in Jordan. I had thought the day might never come; Saddam had always seemed indestructible in a way. He was sentenced to death and executed but he at least had a fair trial, something he denied to countless people who were sentenced to death without justice and summarily executed. My husband may have said something out of turn, I don't know; but my son had done nothing wrong – nothing at all. Both had perished needlessly and unjustly under Saddam's rule. Saddam Hussein had not given a second thought to taking a life, and now his own had been taken. As they say: what goes around, comes around.

I didn't feel a sense of triumph. Strangely, I felt calm and still – I didn't think I would feel like that. I thought I would feel elated but instead I felt like it was the end of an era in Iraq, not just the end of one man's life. I didn't feel sorry for him, just as he had never felt sorry for anyone. My mind flashed back to 1962 when I had first arrived in Iraq and this man was unheard of. I thought of how he had later seemed to be the leader that Iraq needed and that so many people had welcomed, and then of course how the dream had soured and become a living nightmare. I had wanted justice after the secrets, lies and brutality that destroyed my husband and my son and cast a long, dark shadow over my life and my daughter's. Justice has been done. The hatred I once felt for Saddam Hussein has slowly gone. It had to – it was eating away at me, destroying me and I had to let it go. I do feel a sense of peace inside, now that he's dead. Peace, at last.